THE LAO PHRASE BOOK

Samson A. Brier

Edited by
Souphing Saphakdy
Phouphanomlack Sangkhampone

D1720158

Tiny Books

ISBN 974-93612-1-0

First published in 2005 by Tiny Books
6 Sukkasem Road, T. Suthep
Chiang Mai 50200, Thailand

Printed by O.S. Printing House, Bangkok

Contents

Forty-Four Most Common Phrases

1) Hello / I'm fine.
   Sa'baai dii.　　　　　　　　　สะบายดี

2) How are you?
   Jow pen jang daii?　　　　เจ้าเป็นจั่งใด?
   Jow sa'baai dii baww?　　เจ้าสะบายดีบໍ?

3) Thank you (very much).
   Khawp jaii (laai laai).　　ຂอบใจ (ຫลາຍໆ)

4) Never mind.
   Baw pen nyang.　　　　　ບໍ່ເປັນຫຍັງ

5) Do you understand?
   Jow khow jaii baww?　　เจ้าเຂ้าใจบໍ?

6) I (don't) understand.
   Khawy (baw) khow jaii.　　ຂ້ອຍ (ບໍ່) ເຂ້າใจ

7) Wait a minute.
   Jak nawy /　　　　　　จักຫນ່ອຍ/
   Thaa buht nuhng.　　　ຖ້າບິດໜຶ່ງ

8) How much is this?
   An'nii tao daii?　　　　ອັນນີ້ເທ່າใด?

1

9) It's too expensive.
    Paaeng poot.   ແພງໂພດ

10) Can I have a discount?
    Lut daii baww?   ຫຼຸດໄດ້ບໍ?

11) I can (not) discount it.
    Lut (baw) daii.   ຫຼຸດ (ບໍ່) ໄດ້

12) I can, Yes / No
    Daii, Jow/Baww.   ໄດ້, ເຈົ້າ/ບໍ່

13) (No) Good.
    (Baw) dii.   ບໍ່ (ດີ)

14) (Very) Delicious
    Saaep (laai laai).   ແຊບ (ຫລາຍໆ)

15) I'm hungry.
    Khawy hiu khow.   ຂ້ອຍຫິວເຂົ້າ

16) I'm full (already).
    Khawy iim (laae'o).   ຂ້ອຍອີ່ມ (ແລ້ວ)

17) Excuse me.
    Khaww toot.   ຂໍໂທດ

18) What is this in Lao?
    An'nii paa'saa Laao   ອັນນີ້ພາສາລາວແມ່ນຫຍັງ?
    maaen nyang?

19) Do you speak English?
    Jow wow paa'saa ang'git   ເຈົ້າເວົ້າພາສາອັງກິດໄດ້ບໍ?
    daii baww?

2

20) A little.
    Nawy nuhng.   ໜ້ອຍໜຶ່ງ

21) You speak very well.
    Jow wow geng laai.   ເຈົ້າເວົ້າເກ່ງຫຼາຍ

22) What?
    Maaen nyang?   ແມ່ນຫຍັງ?

23) Can you say that again?
    Jow wow iik tuhh'a daii   ເຈົ້າເວົ້າອີກເທື່ອໄດ້ບໍ່?
    baww?

24) Please speak slower.
    Ga'lu'naa wow saa'saa (daae).   ກາລຸນາເວົ້າຊ້າໆ (ແດ່)

25) Finished, gone, done (already).
    Mot (laae'o).   ໝົດ (ແລ້ວ)

26) (I'm) tired.
    (Khawy) muhh'aii.   (ຂ້ອຍ) ເມື່ອຍ

27) It's very hot/cold.
    hawn/now laai.   ຮ້ອນ/ໜາວ ຫຼາຍ

28) Where are you going?
    Jow paii saii?   ເຈົ້າໄປໃສ?

Note: for #28: people might ask "paii saii?" when you walk past
       them, just as they might say "sa'baai dii" (hello). Both are
       casual greetings.

29) Where is the toilet?
   Hawng naam yuu saii?   ຫ້ອງນ້ຳຢູ່ໃສ?

30) Do you have a pen?
   Jow mii bik baww?   ເຈົ້າມີບິກບໍ່?

31) I (don't) have money.
   Khawy (baw) mii ng'n.   ຂ້ອຍ (ບໍ່) ມີເງິນ

32) Do you (want) to drink beer?
   Jow (yaak) duhhm biaa   ເຈົ້າ (ຢາກ) ດື່ມເບຍບໍ່?
   baww?

33) I (don't) want to eat.
   Khawy (baw) yaak gin khow.   ຂ້ອຍ (ບໍ່) ຢາກກິນເຂົ້າ

34) Do you like it spicy?
   Jow mak phet baww?   ເຈົ້າມັກເຜັດບໍ່?

35) I (don't) like blood.
   Khawy (baw) mak luhh'at.   ຂ້ອຍ (ບໍ່) ມັກເລືອດ

36) With(out) chillies,
   (Not) spicy.
   (Baw) saii phet.   (ບໍ່) ໃສ່ເຜັດ

37) What time is it?
   Jak moong (laae'o)?   ຈັກໂມງ (ແລ້ວ) ?

38) Are you happy?
   Jow muan baww?   ເຈົ້າມ່ວນບໍ່?

39) You are very beautiful.
   Jow ngaam laai.   ເຈົ້າງາມຫຼາຍ

40) You are very handsome.
   Jow suu / laww laai.   ເຈົ້າຊູ້/ຫຼໍ່ຫຼາຍ

41) You are also very handsome.
   Jow laww laai kuhh'gan.   ເຈົ້າຫຼໍ່ຫຼາຍຄືກັນ

42) You're more handsome than me.
   Jow laww guaa khawy.   ເຈົ້າຫຼໍ່ກວ່າຂ້ອຍ

43) I love you.
   Khawy hak jow.   ຂ້ອຍຮັກເຈົ້າ

44) Do you love me?
   Jow hak khawy baww?   ເຈົ້າຮັກຂ້ອຍບໍ?

Pronunciation Guide

Vowels

• Lao has some sounds that we do not often hear in English, but do not let this deter you. Listen to the locals for a bit and you will pick it up.

• In Lao, some sounds are short while others are long. Two letters together signifies that the sound is elongated. One "a" for example is short while "aa" warrants a longer sound.

English		Lao
(a)	as in "**ah**"	xະ, xˇ
(aa)	as in "**ahh**"(long)	xๅ
(uh)	as in "**huh!**"	xͦ
(uhh)	as "**huhh**"(long)	xͨ
(i)	as in "**it**"	xͦ
(ii)	as in "**eat**"(long)	xͨ
(u)	as in "fr**u**it"	xຸ
(uu)	as in "y**ou**"(long)	xู
(e)	as in "**egg**"	ເxະ, ເxˇx
(ay, eh)	as in "**day**" or "**hey**" (long)	ເx
(ae)	as in "**a**rrow"	ແxະ, ແxˇະ

6

(aae)	as in "**air**" (long)	แ
(o)	as in "home"	โ
(oo)	as in "**Joe**" (long)	โ
(aw)	as in "**awe!**"	เ
(aww)	as in "**awe**" (long)	อ
(er, uh)	as in "**sir**" at end of words and "**huh**" in the middle.	เ
(err, uhh)	as in "**sir**," sometimes "**huhh**" (long)	เ
(iaa)	as **fiat** (long)	เ (เ)
(uh-a)	as in "**huh**"+ "**ah**"	เ
(uhh-a)	as in "**huhh**" + "**ah**" (long)	เ
(ua)	as in "**whooah!**"	ว
(uua)	as in "**whooah**" (long)	ว
(ia, i'ow)	as in "**idea**"	เ, เ
(iu)	as in "d**ew**ey"	อ
(aii, ai, ai)	as in "**eye**"	ไ, ไ, เ, เ
(short ao, ow; long aao, oww)	as in "**now**"	เ, เ
(aam)	as in "b**om**b"	อ

Special Symbol

• Repeat the sound before ๆ again
example: dtuk ๆ = dtuk dtuk (three-wheeled pick—up truck)

Consonants

• For transliterations with an "**h**" following an initial consonant (ie. "kh") the "**h**" symbolizes an aspiration, otherwise known
as a slight puff of air. Don't worry too much if you don't puff;
people will understand from the context.

(kh)	as in "**k**iss"	ฃ
(k)	as in "**k**ind"	ฅ
(g / k)	as in "**g**ee**k**"	ก (g at beginning, k at end)

• Most guide books and dictionaries use the old French transliteration *k* at the beginning but this writer feels that native English speakers will find that their *g* sound is more appropriate.

| (s) | as in "**s**am" | ซ, ฐ |
| (j) | as in "**j**oy" on roof | จ (tongue slightly back of mouth) |

• This writer also feels that the commonly used transliteration "ch" is inaccurate.

(ng)	as in "ri**ng**"	ง, ญง
(th)	as in "**t**om"	ฏ
(d / t)	as in "**d**o**t**" ฎ (d at beginning, t at end) tongue sightly back on roof of mouth)	
(ph)	as in "**p**ut"	ฝ
(dt)	as in "**d**ead"	ฅ (a combination of a "d" and "t" sound with tongue hitting top-back of top teeth)
(ny / y)	as in "o**ni**on"	ญ (ny at beginning, y at end, ญญ sounds like y in toy)
(fh)	as in "**f**ire"	ฝ, ฟ
(b)	as in "**b**op"	บ (b at beginning, p at end)
(t)	as in "**t**ea"	ฅ
(h)	as in "**h**ome"	ฑ, ร
(p, b)	as in "**p**ie" or "**b**ye") ป (a slight b and p combination sound without aspiration)	
(y)	as in "**y**ellow"	ป

8

(n)	as in "*n*o"	ᚾ, ᚾᚾ
(p)	as in "*p*oor"	ᚹ (no aspiration)
(aw)	as in "long"	ə
(m)	as in "*m*e"	ᚾ, ᚾᚾ
(l)	as in "*l*ike"	ᚨ, ᚾ, ᚾᚨ,
(w)	as in "*w*e"	ɔ (with slight v sound),ᚾɔ
(r)	as in "*r*ed"	ᛋ

Introduction

Enjoy Laos (said *Lao* in-country) and don't worry if you are tone deaf. Speak first, learn the tones later if you wish. People will be happy enough just to speak with you. And when in doubt, speak with a smile.

How to Use This Phrasebook

• English sentences precede their Lao transliteration. The Lao translation follows and the English words in the order they are spoken in Lao are next. The pronunciation guide for the English transliteration can be found on pages 6-9.

• Underlined nouns, adjectives and adverbs can be substituted by other words. Words underlined, or in ( ) are also mirrored in the transliteration and in Lao script so you can find them easily and learn which words mean what as you pick up new phrases.

• In the following example, the word bathroom is underlined in each sentence. Memorize where it belongs and visualize where replacement words such as bus station, bank or moon, etc., would go in its place. Practically every word in the phrasebook, plus hundreds more can be found in the dictionary at the back of the book.

example: Where is the <u>bathroom</u>?
          <u>Hawng naam</u> yuu saii?
          ຫ້ອງນ້ຳຢູ່ໃສ?
          toilet at where

• (Words in parenthesis) can be left out.

Note that although the subjects *I* and *You are* usually omitted in everyday speech they are included here without ( ) for the sake of readability. Hence, in the example below, merely saying *Paii saii?* (Go Where?) is perfectly acceptable and most commonly used.

example: Where are you go(ing)?
          Jow (gamlang) paii saii?
          ເຈົ້າ (ກຳລັງ) ໄປໃສ?
          you (–ing) go where

• / separates two or more exchangeable words to choose from.

example: I will go eat.
          Khawy (si/ja) paii gin khow.
          ຂ້ອຍ (ຊິ/ຈະ) ໄປກິນເຂົ້າ
          I (will) go eat food.

• The Lao script and the visual aides mirror the transliteration underneath.

example: Where are you going?
          Jow (gam lang) (ja/si) paii saii?
          ເຈົ້າ (ກຳລັງ) (ຈະ/ຊິ) ໄປໃສ?
          you (-ing) (will) go where

The following grammar section of this book is a very short, easy introduction to basic Lao. For a more in-depth study of the language, complete with very common and easy to-use grammar parts, refer to *xxiii Grammar* at the back of the book (p. 99).

I. Basic Grammar: The Essentials

Lao word order is very similar to English most of the time, but it does not have as many particles or prepositions.

I	Khawy	ຂ້ອຍ
You	Jow	ເຈົ້າ
(S)he	Laao	ລາວ
You (pl)	Puak jow	ພວກເຈົ້າ
They	Puak khow	ພວກເຂົາ
We	Puak how	ພວກເຮົາ

- **Subject + Verb + Object** is the standard word order.
- TO, A, AN, THE do not exist in Lao.

I am going to eat.
> Khawy (gam lang) paii gin khow.
> I (ing) go eat food

I want to go to the Mekong River.
> Khawy yaak paii Maae naam Khong.
> I want go River Khong

- *To be* is used only with nouns:

(S)he *is* a teacher.	You are pretty.
Laao *pen* aa'jaan.	Jow ngaam.
(S)he *is* teacher	You pretty.

This (thing)	(An) nii	(ອັນ) ນີ້
That/It	(An) nan	(ອັນ) ນັ້ນ
Here	Yuu nii	ຢູ່ນີ້
There	Yuu nan	ຢູ່ນັ້ນ

This is expensive.
　　An'nii paaeng.
　　Thing this expensive

• Adjectives and adverbs follow the noun or adjective, respectively.

You are very <u>handsome</u>.
　　Jow <u>laww</u> laai.
　　You handsome very

This is too <u>expensive</u>.
　　An'nii <u>paaeng</u> poot.
　　Thing this expensive too

• In Lao, if the subject is already known, then leave it out. For example if two men see a pretty woman, there is no need to mention the subject. They might say:

| ngaam | = | pretty |
| ngaam laai | = | very pretty |

• Or maybe you and a friend are bargaining for a tuk-tuk ride or a new shirt. You both already know the subject, so you might say:

| paaeng | = | expensive |
| paaeng poot | = | too expensive |

Asking Questions

When asking a question without question words noitalics *who, what, when, where, why, or how,* you must end the sentence with "*baww*?". Without "*baww*" at the end, the sentence is a statement. "**baww**" at the end of the sentence has a long sound.

This is very <u>delicious.</u>
    An'nii <u>saaep</u> laai.
    Thing this very delicious
    Or: <u>Saaep</u> = Delicious

Is this delicious?
    An'nii saaep **baww?**
    Thing this delicious?
    Or: Saaep **baww?** = Delicious?

• Question words take the place of "baww," most often at the end of the sentence.

<u>Who</u> *is* he?
    Laao <u>maaen pai</u>**?**
    He is who

<u>What</u> is this?
    An'nii <u>maaen nyang</u>**?**
    Thing this is what

<u>Where</u> is the toilet?
    Hawng naam <u>yuu saii?</u>
    Toilet is where

<u>When</u> is the bus leaving?
(<u>What time</u> is the bus leaving?)
    Lot meh awwk <u>jak moong</u>**?**
    Bus go out what time

Why?

Pen nyang?

How do you say this in Lao?

An'nii (jow) wow (pen) paa'saa Lao naaeo dai?

thing this (you) say (is) language Lao how

• Finally, there are many forms of "yes". The most common polite form is **Jow**.

Jow is good for any occasion, with anyone.

Yes, (I am from Iceland).

Jow ເຈົ້າ.

Daii is used to show ability, for example, Yes I can.

Yes, I can (speak Lao).

Daii ໄດ້.

Uhh is common between friends or people who are friendly toward each other. It is similar to "uh huh" or "yeah."

Maen laae'o means "that's right."

Doy and **Doy kha'nawy** are used when talking to monks or high officials and sometimes in respect to one's elders.

From most casual to most polite forms of "yes":

Uhh, Maen laae'o, Jow, Doy, Doy kha'nawy

ເອີ, ແມ່ນ ແລ້ວ, ເຈົ້າ, ໂດຍ, ໂດຍຂະນ້ອຍ

There is only one "no" and alone its sound is long: Baww ບໍ່

II. Twenty-nine Common Questions & Answers

1) How are you?
> Jow pen jang daii? (informal)
> ເຈົ້າເປັນຈັ່ງໃດ?
> Jow sa'baai dii baww? (polite)
> ເຈົ້າສະບາຍດີບໍ່?

Fine, and you?
> Sa'baai dii, (Laae) jow deh?
> ສະບາຍດີ (ແລະ) ເຈົ້າເດ?

I'm fine (also).
> Khawy sa'baai dii (kuhh'gan)
> ຂ້ອຍສະບາຍດີ (ຄືກັນ)

Thank you (very much).
> Khawp jaii (laai laai)
> ຂອບໃຈ (ຫຼາຍໆ)

2) Where are you going?
> Jow paii saii?
> ເຈົ້າໄປໃສ?
> You go where

I'm going to the <u>market.</u>
　　Khawy paii <u>dta'laat.</u>
　　ຂ້ອຍໄປຕະຫຼາດ
　　I go market

3) How much?
　　Tao daii?
　　ເທົ່າໃດ?

4) Can I have a discount?
　　Lut daii baww?
　　ຫຼຸດໄດ້ບໍ່?
　　discount can

Note: See 'Bargaining' on page 29 for better tactics.

5) What's your name?
　　Jow suhh nyang?
　　ເຈົ້າຊື່ຫຍັງ?
　　you name what

　　My name is <u>Nawy.</u>
　　Khawy suhh <u>Nawy.</u>
　　ຂ້ອຍຊື່ນ້ອຍ
　　I name Nawy

6) Where are you from?
　　Jow maa jaak/dtaae saii?
　　ເຈົ້າມາຈາກ/ແຕ່ໃສ?
　　you come from where

　　What nationality are you?
　　Jow pen kon pa'teht daii?
　　ເຈົ້າເປັນຄົນປະເທດໃດ?
　　you are person country

Countries

I'm (a/an) . . . . .   I'm from . . . . .
  Khawy pen kon . . . . .   Khawy maa jaak/dtaae . . . . .
  ຂ້ອຍເປັນຄົນ . . . .   ຂ້ອຍມາຈາກ/ແຕ່ . . . .

Note: In Lao, the country and the adjectival form are the same word. For example. I'm English and I'm from England both use the same word: England.

Africa	aa'fhiik'gaa	ອາຟຼິກກາ
Australia	ot's(a)'dtaa'lii	ອົດສະຕາລີ
Canada	kaae naa daa	ແຄນາດາ
Belgium	biao yiam	ເບວຢ້ຽມ
China	jiin	ຈີນ
Denmark	den maak	ເດັນມາກ
England	ang'git	ອັງກິດ
France	fha'lang	ຝະລັ່ງ
Germany	yiaa la man	ເຢຍລະມັນ
Holland	hoon lang	ໂຮນລັງ
Hong Kong	hong gong	ຮ່ອງກົງ
India	in diaa	ອິນເດຍ
Israel	iis raa'ayl	ອິສຣາເອລ
Italy	ii'dtaa'lii	ມີຕາລີ
Japan	nyii pun	ຍີ່ປຸ່ນ
Laos	laao	ລາວ
New Zealand	niu sii laaen	ນິວຊີແລນ
Singapore	sing ga poo	ສິງກະໂປ
Spain	s(a) payn	ສະປນ
Sweden	s(a) wii den	ສະວິເດັນ
Switzerland	swit serr laaen	ສວິດເຊີແລນ
Taiwan	dtaii wan	ໄຕ້ຫວັນ
USA	aa'may'li'gaa	ອາເມລິກາ

Hi and Bye

7) Where have you just been?
(sometimes this means "where are you from?"
> Jow maa dtaae saii?
> ເຈົ້າມາແຕ່ໃສ?
> you come from where

I just came from the <u>post office.</u>
> Khawy maa dtaae <u>Hawng gaan paii'sa'nii.</u>
> ຂ້ອຍມາແຕ່ຫ້ອງການໄປສະນີ
> I come from post office

8) See you.
> Pop gan maii . . . . .
> ພົບກັນໃໝ່. . . . .

later	oo gaat na	ໂອກາດໜ້າ
tomorrow	muh uhhn	ມື້ອື່ນ
this weekend	taai aa'titnii	ທ້າຍອາທິດນີ້

9) Goodbye
laa gawn	(if you leave first)	ລາກ່ອນ
paii gawn	(if you leave first)	ໄປກ່ອນ
sook dii	(if you don't leave or are second to do so)	ໂຊກດີ

10) Can you speak <u>Lao</u>?
> Jow wow paa'saa <u>Laao</u> daii baww?
> ເຈົ້າເວົ້າພາສາ<u>ລາວ</u>ໄດ້ບໍ່?
> you say speak Laao can

No.	baww (daii).	ບໍ່ (ໄດ້) not (able)
A little.	nawy nuhng.	ໜ້ອຍໜຶ່ງ
Not much.	baww laai (paan daii).	ບໍ່ຫຼາຍ (ປານໃດ)
I'm fluent.	khawy wow daii sombuun.	ຂ້ອຍເວົ້າໄດ້ສົມບູນ
(And) you?	(laae) jow daae?	(ແລະ) ເຈົ້າແດ່?

11) This is my <u>friend</u>.

Nii maaen <u>muu</u> (khawng) khawy.

ນີ້ແມ່ນໝູ່ <u>(ຂອງ)</u> ຂ້ອຍ

This is friend (of) me

Note: Friend (muu) can easily be confused with pig (mu); (khawng) is a possessive marker.

husband	pu'aa	ຜົວ
wife	miaa	ເມຍ
son	luuk saai	ລູກຊາຍ
daughter	luuk saao	ລູກສາວ
brother (younger/ older)	nawng saai/aai	ນ້ອງຊາຍ/ອ້າຍ
sister (younger/ older)	nawng saao/uhh'aai	ນ້ອງສາວ/ເອື້ອຍ

12) How old are you?

Jow aa'nyu jak pii?

ເຈົ້າອາຍຸຈັກປີ?

you age how many years

I am 20 years old.

Khawy aa'nyu <u>saao</u> pii.

ຂ້ອຍອາຍຸ<u>ສາວ</u>ປີ

I age 20 years

Really? So <u>young/old</u>!

Taae waa? <u>num/thow</u> kha'naat naw!

ແທ້ຫວ່າ? ໜຸ່ມ/ເຖົ້າ ຂະໜາດເນາະ

Calculting ages:

1	(et)	8	(paaet)
2	(sawng)	9	(gao)
3	(saam)	10	(sip)
4	(sii)	20	(saao)
5	(haa)	30	(saam sip)
6	(hok)	40	(sii sip)
7	(jet),	50	(haa sip)

For example, 19 = sip gao, 25 = saao haa, 31 = saam sip et, 44 = sii sip sii. (See p. 97 for help with numbers).

13) How long have you been in Laos?

Jow yuu Laao don (paan dai) laae'o?

ເຈົ້າຢູ່ລາວດົນ (ປານ ໃດ) ແລ້ວ?

you in Laos how long already

<u>3</u> days / weeks / months / years / forever

<u>Saam</u> muhh / aa'tit /duhh'an /pii /dtalawt baii

ສາມມື້ / ອາທິດ / ເດືອນ / ປີ / ຕະຫຼອດໄປ

14) How much longer will you be in Laos?

Jow ja yuu Laao iik don (paan) daii ?

ເຈົ້າຈະຢູ່ລາວອີກດົນ (ປານ) ໃດ?

you will be in Laos again how much longer

2 more <u>weeks</u>.

iik sawng <u>aa'tit.</u>

ອີກ 2 <u>ອາທິດ</u>

About 2 <u>months</u>.
Pa'maan sawng <u>duhh'an.</u>
ปะมาม 2 ເດືອນ

15) Do you like it here?
Jow mak yuu nii baww?
ເຈົ້າມັກຢູ່ນີ້ບໍ່
you like here this?

Yes / I love it / I sure do / Yeah
Jow / Khawy mak laai / Maaen laae'o / Uhh
ເຈົ້າ / ຂ້ອຍມັກຫຼາຍ / ແມ່ນ / ເອີ

16) Where are you staying / living now?
Di'ow nii jow pak yuu saii?
ຕອນນີ້ເຈົ້າພັກຢູ່ໃส?
now you stay at where

Now, I'm staying at . . . . .
Di'ow nii khawy pak yuu . . . . .
ຕອນນີ້ຂ້ອຍພັກຢູ່ . . . . .
now I stay at . . . . .

17) What's your *phone number*?
Naamber too la sap khawng jow maaen nyang?
ນ້າເບີໂທລະສັບຂອງເຈົ້າແມ່ນຫຍັງ?
number phone of you is what

18) <u>Do you want</u> to go with me?
<u>Jow yaak</u> paii gap khawy baww?
ເຈົ້າຢາກໄປກັບຂ້ອຍບໍ່?
you want go with I

23

Yes / OK.

> Jow / OoKay.
> ເຈົ້າ / ໂອເຄ

I don't have time.

> Khawy baw mii way'laa
> ຂ້ອຍບໍ່ມີເວລາ
> I no have time

19) Are you a <u>tourist</u>?

> Jow maaen <u>nak tawng ti'ow</u> baww?
> ເຈົ້າແມ່ນນັກທ່ອງທ່ຽວບໍ?
> you are tourist

Yes: Jow ເຈົ້າ   No: Baww ບໍ່

I'm here on <u>business.</u>

> Khawy maaen <u>nak tu la git</u> yuu nii.
> ຂ້ອຍແມ່ນນັກທຸລະກິດຢູ່ນີ້
> I is business at here

I <u>work</u> here.

> Khawy <u>het wiak</u> yuu nii.
> ຂ້ອຍເຮັດວຽກຢູ່ນີ້
> I work at here

20) Do you like Lao <u>women/men</u>?

> Jow mak <u>phuu nying/phuu sai</u> Laao baww?
> ເຈົ້າມັກ ຜູ້ຍິງ/ຜູ້ຊາຍ ລາວບໍ?
> you like <u>woman/man</u> Lao

very pretty	ngaam laai	ງາມຫຼາຍ
handsome	jow suu, laww	ເຈົ້າຊູ້, ຫຼໍ່
nice, good	dii	ດີ

21) Are you married?

Jow dtaaeng ngaan laaéo baww?

ເຈົ້າແຕ່ງງານແລ້ວບໍ?

you married already

Yes	Jow	ເຈົ້າ
Not yet:	Nyang tuhh'a	ຍັງເທື່ອ

22) Do you have a girlfriend/boyfriend?

Jow mii fhaaen laae´o baww?

ເຈົ້າມີແຟນແລ້ວບໍ?

you have girlfriend/boyfriend already

Yes: Jow ເຈົ້າ   No: Baww ບໍ່

23) Is (s)he Lao?

Laao maaen kon laao baww?

ລາວແມ່ນຄົນລາວບໍ?

(s)he is person Lao

Yes: Jow ເຈົ້າ   No: Baww ບໍ່

24) Do you like Beer Lao?

Jow mak biaa Laao baww?

ເຈົ້າມັກເບຍລາວບໍ?

you like beer Lao

Yes/ Of course / Yeah

Jow / Naae nawn / Maaen laae'o.

ເຈົ້າ / ແນ່ນອນ / ແມ່ນແລ້ວ

I don't drink alcohol.

Khawy baw duhm aae'o'gaww' haww.

ຂ້ອຍບໍ່ດື່ມເຫຼົ້າກໍ່ຣໍ່

I no drink alcohol

I only drink <u>Lao whiskey</u>.

Khawy duhm piang dtaae Laao Lao (Lao special whiskey).

ຂ້ອຍດື່ມພຽງແຕ່ເຫລົ້າລາວ

I drink only whiskey Lao

25) Do you like <u>Lao food</u>?

Jow mak <u>aa'haan Laao</u> baww?

ເຈົ້າມັກ<u>ອາຫານລາວ</u>ບໍ່?

you like food Lao?

Yes / I sure do.

Jow / Maaen laae´o

ເຈົ້າ / ແມ່ນແລ້ວ

26) Have you been to <u>Luang Prabang</u>?

Jow kuhh'y paii <u>Luang Pabaang</u> laae'o baww?

ເຈົ້າເຄີຍໄປ<u>ຫລວງພະບາງ</u>ແລ້ວບໍ່?

you have been go Luang Prabang already

Yes / Not yet.

Jow / Nyang tuhh'a.

ເຈົ້າ / ຍັງເທື່ອ

27) How many people are in your <u>family</u>?

Yuu naii <u>kawp ku'a</u> jow mii jak kon?

ຢູ່ໃນ<u>ຄອບຄົວ</u>ເຈົ້າມີຈັກຄົນ?

in family your have how many people

I have two <u>older brothers</u>.

Khawy mii <u>aai</u> sawng kon.

ຂ້ອຍມີ<u>ອ້າຍ</u>ສອງຄົນ

I have older brother 2 people

I have one <u>younger sister.</u>

Khawy mii <u>nawg saao</u> kon nuhng.

ຂ້ອຍມີນ້ອງສາວຄົນໜຶ່ງ

I have younger sister girl person one

I am an only child.

Khawy maaen luuk toon.

ຂ້ອຍແມ່ນລູກໂທນ

I am child on

28) Do you have <u>children?</u>

Jow mii <u>luk</u> baww?

ເຈົ້າມີລູກບໍ່?

you have child little

Yes	Jow	ເຈົ້າ
No	Baww	ບໍ່
Not yet	Nyang tuhh'a	ຍັງເທື່ອ

Jobs

29) What do you do?

Jow het wiak nyang?

ເຈົ້າເຮັດວຽກຫຍັງ?

you work what?

I am a/an . . . . .

Khawy pen . . . . .

ຂ້ອຍເປັນ . . . . .

accountant	ban'sii	ບັນຊີ
actor	nak sa'daaeng	ນັກສະແດງ
artist	nak dtaaem	ນັກແຕ້ມ
bartender	kon pung laao	ຄົນປຸງເຫລົ້າ

bodyguard	kon kum kawng	ຄົນຄຸ້ມຄອງ
brain surgeon	maww pu'aa sa'mawng	ໝໍ່ປົວສະໝອງ
cook	paww ku'aa	ພໍ່ຄົວ
doctor	taan maww	ທ່ານໝໍ
engineer	wi sa'wa gawn	ວິດສະວະກອນ
farmer	saao naa	ຊາວນາ
kick-boxer	nak mu'aii	ນັກມວຍ
lawyer	nak got naai	ນັກກົດໝາຍ
musician	nak don dtii	ນັກດົນຕີ
I sell	khawy khaai . . .	ຂ້ອຍຂາຍ. . . . .
student	nak hian	ນັກຮຽນ
teacher	aa'jaan, naai kuu	ອາຈານ, ນາຍຄູ
volunteer	aa'saa sa'mak	ອາສາສະໝັກ

III. Bargaining

1) How much is <u>this</u>?
   <u>An'nii</u> tao daii?
   ອັນນີ້ເທົ່າໃດ?
   thing this how much

2) It's (very) <u>expensive.</u>
   <u>Paaeng</u> (laai).
   ແພງ (ຫຼາຍ)
   expensive (very)

3) Can I have a discount?
   Lut daii baww?
   ຫຼຸດໄດ້ບໍ?
   discount can?

   No, You can't have a discount.
   Lut baw daii.
   ຫຼຸດບໍ່ໄດ້
   discount no can

   Yes. You can have a discount.
   Lut daii.
   ຫຼຸດໄດ້
   discount can

If a vendor says "Lut daii," you should suggest a new price.

4) I don't have enough <u>money</u>.
   Khawy mii <u>ng'n</u> baw paww.
   ຂ້ອຍມີເງິນບໍ່ພໍ
   I have money no enough

5) Do you have anything <u>cheaper</u>?
   Jow mii an <u>thuhhk gu'aa</u> nii baww?
   ເຈົ້າມີອັນຖືກກວ່ານີ້ບໍ?
   you have thing cheaper (than) this?

6) How much if I buy <u>two</u>?
   Thaa khawy suhh <u>sawng</u> an laak'kaa tao daii?
   ຖ້າຂ້ອຍຊື້ສອງອັນລາຄາເທົ່າໃດ?
   if I buy two things price will how much

7) Never mind.
   Baww pen nyang.
   ບໍ່ເປັນຫຍັງ

8) Where is a <u>bank</u>?
   Ta'naa'kaan yuu saii?
   ທະນາຄານຢູ່ໃສ?
   bank at where

All mini-marts serve as handy places to exchange Dollars or Baht at the market rate, which is generally a bit better than the bank rate.

9) Exchange <u>rate</u>
   At'dtaa laaek pian
   ອັດຕາແລກປ່ຽນ
   rate exchange

10) Lao Kip

kip

ກີບ

11) US Dollars

doo'laa

ໂດລາ

12) Thai Baht

Baat

ບາດ

13) Do you change <u>Dollars/Baht</u>?

Jow hap pian <u>doo'laa/baat</u> baww?

ເຈົ້າຮັບປ່ຽນ<u>ໂດລາ/ບາດ</u> ບໍ?

you accept change dollars / baht

14) What is the exchange rate <u>for Dollars to Kip/Baht to Kip</u>?

At dtaa <u>doolaa kip/baat kip</u> tao daii?

ອັດຕາໂດລາເປັນ ກີບ/ບາດ ເປັນກີບເທົ່າໃດ?

rate dollar to Kip/Baht to kip how much

15) Do you cash <u>traveler's checks</u>?

Jow hap pian <u>sek tawng ti'ow</u> baww?

ເຈົ້າຮັບປ່ຽນ<u>ເຊັກທ່ອງທ່ຽວ</u>ບໍ?

you take change traveler's checks

16) Bank <u>rate</u>

<u>At'dtaa</u> ta'naa'kaan

<u>ອັດຕາ</u>ທະນາຄານ

rate bank

17) Black <u>market</u> rate

    At'dtaa <u>dta'laat</u> muhht

    ອັຕຕາ<u>ຕະຫຼາດ</u>ມືດ

    rate market dark

18) Do you have <u>bigger</u> notes?

    Jow mii baii <u>nyaii gu'aa</u> nii baww?

    ເຈົ້າມີໃບໃຫຍ່<u>ຍກວ່າ</u>ນີ້ບໍ່?

    you have paper bigger (than) this?

2,000 and 5,000 Kip notes were introduced in the late 1990s but they did not keep up with inflation, hence 10,000 and 20,000 Kip notes entered into circulation in 2001. The other notes making the rounds are the 1,000, 500, 100 and 50. To help put things in perspective, the exchange rate in the early 1990s was 700 Kip to one Dollar; in 2004 it is over 10,000 to one. A bottle of Beer Lao costs about 7,000 Kip at an outdoor bar and an hour at the Internet costs 6,000.

IV. Guesthouses

Finding a Room

1) Do you have any <u>rooms</u> available?
   Jow mii <u>hawng</u> waang baww?
   ເຈົ້າມີ<u>ຫ້ອງ</u>ຫວ່າງບໍ?
   you have room available

   There are no rooms <u>available.</u>
   Baw mii <u>(hawng waang)</u> (luhh'y)
   ບໍ່ມີ <u>(ຫ້ອງຫວ່າງ)</u> (ເລີຍ)
   no have (room available) (emphasis)

   It's <u>full</u> already.
   <u>Dtem</u> laae'o
   ເຕັມແລ້ວ
   full already

2) How many <u>people</u>?
   Mii jak <u>kon</u>?
   ມີຈັກ<u>ຄົນ</u>?
   have how many person

3) There are 2 of <u>us.</u>
   <u>Pu'ak how</u> mii sawng kon.
   ພວກເຮົາມີສອງຄົນ
   we have 2 people

33

4) Do you have a room with ..... ?
>   Jow mii hawng nawn gap ..... baww?
>   ເຈົ້າມີຫ້ອງນອນກັບ ..... ບໍ່?
>   you have room sleep with .....

a/c (air)	aae	ແອ
one big bed	dtiang nyaii dtiang nuhng	ຕຽງໃຫຍ່ຕຽງໜຶ່ງ
two beds	sawng dtiang	ສອງຕຽງ
a shower	fak bu'aa	ຝັກບົວ
hot water	naam hawn	ນ້ຳຮ້ອນ
a fan	pat lom	ພັດລົມ

5) Do you have anything <u>cheaper</u>?
>   Jow mii baaep uhhn tii (laa'kaa) <u>thuhhk gu'aa</u> nii baww?
>   ເຈົ້າມີແບບອື່ນທີ່ (ລາຄາ) <u>ຖືກກວ່າ</u>ນີ້ບໍ່?
>   you have same as this (price) cheap-er this?

6) I'd like the <u>cheapest</u> room you've got.
>   Khawy yaak daii hawng tii <u>thuhhk tii sut.</u>
>   ຂ້ອຍຢາກໄດ້ຫ້ອງທີ່<u>ຖືກທີ່ສຸດ</u>
>   I want room at cheapest

7) Can <u>I/we</u> see it?
>   <u>Khawy/Puak how</u> khaw b´ng daii baww?
>   <u>ຂ້ອຍ/ພວກເຮົາ</u>ຂໍເບິ່ງໄດ້ບໍ່?
>   I/we please look at can?

8) Where's the <u>elevator</u>?
>   <u>Lip</u> yuu saii?
>   <u>ລິບ</u>ຢູ່ໃສ?
>   lift at where

9) Do you have a <u>card</u> with the hotel's name and number on it?
Jow mii <u>naam'bat</u> hoong haaem baww?
ເຈົ້າມີ<u>ນາມບັດ</u>ໂຮງແຮມບໍ່?
you have name card hotel

10) Can I use the <u>phone</u>, please?
Khaww saii <u>too'la'sap</u> dai baww?
ຂໍໃຊ້<u>ໂທລະສັບ</u>ໄດ້ບໍ່ ?
please use telephone can

11) Do you <u>change</u> money ?
Jow <u>hap pian</u> ng´n baww?
ເຈົ້າ<u>ຮັບປ່ຽນ</u>ເງິນບໍ່?
you change money

12) Do you rent <u>bikes/motorbikes</u>?
Jow haii sao <u>lot thiip/lot jak</u> baww?
ເຈົ້າໃຫ້ເຊົ່າ <u>ລົດຖີບ/ລົດຈັກ</u> ບໍ່?
you give rent bicycle / motor bike

13) Where can I <u>wash (my) clothes</u>?
Khawy <u>sak kuhh'ang (khawy)</u> daii yuu saii?
ຂ້ອຍ<u>ຊັກເຄື່ອງ</u> (ຂ້ອຍ) ໄດ້ຢູ່ໃສ?
I wash clothes of I can where

14) Do you do laundry?
Jow hap sak kuhh'ang baww?
ເຈົ້າຮັບຊັກເຄື່ອງບໍ່?
you take wash clothes

15) When will it be ready?
Man ja laae'o dtawn daii?
ມັນຈະແລ້ວຕອນໃດ?
it will already when

16) Do you have (another).....?

    Jow mii .....(iik) baww?

    ເຈົ້າມີ ..... (ອີກ) ບໍ່?

    you have ....another ?

blanket	phaa hom	ຜ້າຮົ່ມ
conditioner	kiim nuat phom	ຄີມນວດຜົມ
detergent	fhaaep	ແຟບ
iron	dtow liit	ເຕົາລີດ
pillow	mawn	ມອນ
razor	miit thaae'muat	ມີດແຖບໜວດ
shampoo	yaa sa'phom	ຍາສະຜົມ
shaving cream	foom thaae'muat	ໂຟມແຖບໜວດ
soap	sa'buu	ສະບູ
towel	phaa'set dtoo	ຜ້າເຊັດໂຕ

17) Do you sell ..... ?

    Jow khaai ..... baww?

    ເຈົ້າຂາຍ.....ບໍ່?

    you sell ..... ?

cold water	naam yen	ນ້ຳເຢັນ
Pepsi	pep sii	ເປັບຊີ
Coke	kook	ໂຄກ
maps	paaen tii	ແຜນທີ່
stamps	sa'dtaaem	ສະແຕມ

18) Where is the <u>trash can</u>?

    <u>Thang khii nyuhh'a</u> yuu saii ?

    ຖັງຂີ້ເຫຍື້ອຢູ່ໃສ?

    trashcan have at where

19) I/we want to stay <u>one</u> more night.
    <u>Khawy/puak how</u> yaak pak iik <u>nuhhng</u> kuhhn.
    <u>ຂ້ອຍ/ພວກເຮົາ</u>ຢາກພັກອີກ<u>ໜຶ່ງ</u>ຄືນ
    I/we want stay another one night

20) I'd like to <u>change</u> rooms.
    Khawy dtawng gaan <u>pian</u> hawng.
    ຂ້ອຍຕ້ອງການປ່ຽນຫ້ອງ
    I want change room

21) I'd like to check out.
    Sek ow ເຊັກເອົາ   (I'd like to check out).
    Gep ng´n ເກັບເງິນ (How much do I owe?)

22) Can I have a <u>receipt</u>?
    Khaww <u>bin</u> daae?
    ຂໍບິນແດ່?
    may check please

23) There is a <u>mistake</u>.
    Jow laii ng´n haii khawy <u>phit</u>
    ເຈົ້າໄລ່ເງິນໃຫ້ຂ້ອຍຜິດ
    You check money give me mistake

24) Can I leave my <u>bags</u> here?
    Khawy faak <u>ga'bow</u> daii baww?
    ຂ້ອຍຝາກກະເປົາໄດ້ບໍ?
    I leave bag can

V. Phone, Post, Fax & Email

Phone

1) Where is the <u>phone/post office</u>?
   Too'la'sap/paii'sa'nii yuu saii?
   ໂທລະສັບ/ໄປສະນີ ຢູ່ໃສ?
   telephone/PO at where

2) Can I make a collect call?
   Khawy khaww too sia paai taang daii baww?
   ຂ້ອຍຂໍໂທເສຍປາຍທາງໄດ້ບໍ?
   I may call pay end way can

3) Do you have <u>phone cards</u>?
   Jow mii <u>bat too'la'sap</u> baww?
   ເຈົ້າມີບັດໂທລະສັບບໍ?
   you have card phone

4) What is the <u>phone number</u> here?
   Berr <u>too'la'sap</u> yuu nii tow daii?
   ເບີໂທລະສັບຢູ່ນີ້ເທົ່າໃດ?
   number phone at here how much

address	tii yuu	ທີ່ຢູ່
fax number	berr fhaaek	ເບີ ແຟກ

5) How much is it to make a(n) <u>international/local</u> call?

    Too <u>paai nawk/naii</u> tow daii?

    ໂທພາຍນອກ/ໃນ ເທົ່າໃດ?

    call international/local how much

Post, Fax and Email

1) How much is it to <u>call England</u>?

    <u>Too paii ang'git</u> tao daii?

    ໂທໄປອັງກິດເທົ່າໃດ?

    call go England how much

fax	fhaaek	ແຟກ
send a postcard to.....	song gak paii	ສົ່ງລັມໄປ.....
send this	song an'nii	ສົ່ງລັມນີ້
email	ii'may'o	ອີເມວ

2) How much per <u>page/minute/hour</u>?

    Laa'kaa tao daii <u>dtaww naa/naa tii/su'aa moong</u> nuhng?

    ລາຄາເທົ່າໃດ ຕໍ່ໜ້າ/ນາທີ/ຊົ່ວໂມງ ໜຶ່ງ?

    price how much page/min/hour one

3) Can I see the <u>stamps</u>?

    Khawy b´ng <u>sa'dtaaem</u> daii baww?

    ຂ້ອຍເບິ່ງສະແຕມໄດ້ບໍ່?

    I look at stamps can

4) Do you have a <u>pen</u>?

    Jow mii <u>bik</u> baww?

    ເຈົ້າມີບິກບໍ່?

    you have pen

boxes	dtuu waang	ຕູ້ຫວ່າງ
envelopes	sawng jot maai	ຊອງຈົດໝາຍ
paper	jia	ເຈ້ຍ
postcards	gak	ກັກ
stamps	sa'dtaaem	ສະແຕມ

Sample Phone Conversation

a) Is Sam there?

> Sam yuu baww?
> ແຊມຢູ່ບໍ່?
> sam at

b) Yes. Wait a minute.

> Jow. Jak nawy / Thaa buht nuhng / Thaa buht di'ow.
> ເຈົ້າ. ຈັກໜ່ອຍ / ຖ້າບຶດໜຶ່ງ / ຖ້າບຶດດຽວ
> yes. wait a second

  No, (s)he's not here.

> Baw yuu.
> ບໍ່ຢູ່
> no at

a) When will (s)he <u>be back</u>?

> Laao ja <u>gap'maa</u> muhh'a daii?
> ລາວຈະ<u>ກັບມາ</u>ເມື່ອໃດ?
> (s)he will return come when

b) At <u>3:00</u>/ I don't know.

> <u>Saam moong</u> / Baw huu.
> <u>ສາມໂມງ</u> / ບໍ່ຮູ້
> 3:00 time / no know

a)   Where is <u>(s)he</u>?
     <u>Laao</u> yuu saii?
     ລາວຢູ່ໃສ?
     (s)he at where

b)   (S)he is at <u>school</u>. / I don't know.
     Laao yuu <u>hoong hian</u> / Baw huu.
     ລາວຢູ່<u>ໂຮງຮຽນ</u> / ບໍ່ຮູ້
     (s)he at school / no know

a)   Does (S)he have a mobile phone?
     Laao mii muhh tuh baww?
     ລາວມີມືຖື່ບໍ່
     (s)he have mobile phone

b)   No, (s)he doesn't have.
     Baw mii
     ບໍ່ມີ
     no have

a)   Can I leave a message?
     Khawy khaww fhaak <u>khaww kuaam</u> daii baww?
     ຂ້ອຍຂໍຝາກ<u>ຂໍ້ຄວາມ</u>ໄດ້ບໍ່?
     I may leave message can ?

b)   OK. Wait a second.
     Daii. Jak nawy/Thaa buht nuhng.
     ໄດ້. ຈັກໜ່ອຍ/ຖ້າບິດໜຶ່ງ
     can. wait a second

     What's your <u>name</u>?
     Jow <u>suhh</u> nyang?
     ເຈົ້າ<u>ຊື່</u>ຫຍັງ?
     you name what

a) My name is <u>Sam</u>.

    Khawy suhh <u>Sam</u>.

    ຂ້ອຍຊື່ແຊມ

    I name Sam

Tell him/her that to <u>call</u> me please.

    Bawk laao hai <u>too'haa</u> khawy daae.

    ບອກລາວໃຫ້ໂທຫາຂ້ອຍແດ່

    tell him/her give call me please

My number is .....

    Berr too'la'sap khawy maaen.....

    ເບີໂທລະສັບຂ້ອຍແມ່ນ

    number phone mine is .....

I'm in room .....

    Khawy yuu naii hawng .....

    ຂ້ອຍຢູ່ໃນຫ້ອງ .....

    I at in room .....

Thank you.

    Khawp jaii.

    ຂອບໃຈ

vi. Travel

Getting to & around Laos

1) I'd like a tourist <u>visa</u>.
   Khawy dtawng gaan <u>wii'saa</u> tawng ti'ow.
   ຂ້ອຍຕ້ອງການ<u>ວີຊາ</u>ທ່ອງທ່ຽວ
   I want visa tourist

2) Is this the <u>bus</u> to Laos? (Coming from Thailand)
   Nii maaen <u>lot meh</u> paii Laao baww?
   ນີ້ແມ່ນ<u>ລົດເມ</u>ໄປລາວບໍ່?
   this is bus go Lao

3) What time (will) the bus <u>leave</u>?
   Lot (ja) <u>awwk</u> jak moong?
   ລົດ (ຈະ) <u>ອອກ</u>ຈັກໂມງ?
   bus (will) leave what time

4) How much is it?
   Tao daii?
   ເທົ່າໃດ?
   how much

5) How much to <u>Vientiane</u>?
   Paii Wiang Jan (laa'kaa) tao daii?
   ໄປ<u>ວຽງຈັນ</u> (ລາຄາ) ເທົ່າໃດ?
   go Vientiane (price) how much

43

6) That's too expensive.
   Paaeng poot.
   ແພງໂພດ
   expensive too

7) OK (in agreement).
   Dtok long.
   ຕົກລົງ

Extending Visa

1) Where is <u>Immigration</u>?
   <u>Gom gu'at kon khow muhh'ang</u> yuu saii?
   <u>ກົມກວດຄົນເຂົ້າເມືອງ</u>ຢູ່ໃສ?
   immigration where is

2) I'd like to extend my visa.
   Khawy dtawng'gaan dtaww wii'saa khawng khawy.
   ຂ້ອຍຕ້ອງການຕໍ່ວິຊາຂອງຂ້ອຍ
   I need extend visa of mine

3) Do you accept Baht/<u>Dollars</u>?
   Jow hap ng´n baat/<u>doo'laa</u> baww?
   ເຈົ້າຮັບເງິນ ບາດ/<u>ໂດລາ</u> ບໍ່
   you take money Baht/Dollars?

4) When will it be ready?
   Man ja laae'o dtawn daii?
   ມັນຈະແລ້ວຕອນໃດ?
   it will already finish can

5) What time do you <u>open/close</u>?
   Jow <u>buhht/bit</u> baan jak moong?
   ເຈົ້າ <u>ເປີດ/ປິດ</u> ບ້ານຈັກໂມງ?
   you open/close house what time

6) Do you speak <u>English</u>?
   Jow wow paa'saa <u>ang'git</u> daii baww?
   ເຈົ້າເວົ້າພາສາ<u>ອັງກິດ</u>ໄດ້ບໍ່?
   you speak language English able

English	ang'git	ອັງກິດ
Japanese	nyii'pun	ຍີ່ປຸ່ນ
French	fha'lang	ຝະລັ່ງ
Chinese	jiin	ຈີນ

Getting out of Town

1) Where is the bus to ..... ?
   Lot meh paii ..... yuu saii?
   ລົດເມໄປ ..... ຢູ່ໃສ?
   bus go ..... at where

2) What time does the bus to ..... leave?
   Jak moong lot meh ja awwk paii .....?
   ຈັກໂມງລົດເມຈະອອກໄປ ..... ?
   what time bus will leave go .....

3) I'd like two bus tickets.
   Khawy dtawng gaan pii lot sawng pii.
   ຂ້ອຍຕ້ອງການປີ້ລົດສອງປີ້
   I want ticket bus 2 tickets

4) Where is the <u>bus/toilet</u>?

Lot'meh/hawng naam yuu saii?

ລົດເມ/ຫ້ອງນ້ຳຢູ່ໃສ?

bus/toilet at where

5) How long does it take?

Dtawng saii way'laa <u>don'paan'daii</u>?

ຕ້ອງໃຊ້ເວລາດົນປານໃດ?

must use time how long

6) When does it <u>leave/arrive</u>?

Muhh'a daii ja <u>paii/hawt</u>?

ເມື່ອໃດຈະ<u>ໄປ/ຮອດ</u>?

when will go/arrive

7) It's full.

Dtem laae'o.

ເຕັມແລ້ວ

8) When is the <u>next</u> bus?

Lot'meh <u>thi'ow dtaww paii</u> maaen jak moong?

ລົດເມ<u>ທີ່ອວຕໍ່ໄປ</u>ແມ່ນຈັກໂມງ?

bus next is what time

9) How much is it to fly to ..... ?

Pii nyon ..... (laa'kaa) tao daii?

ປີ້ຍົນ..... (ລາຄາ) ເທົ່າໃດ?

ticket plane go ..... (price) how much

Transport Dilemmas

1) Do you have <u>motion sickness medicine</u>?
   Jow mii <u>yaa gan haak</u> baww?
   ເຈົ້າມີຢາກັນຮາກບໍ່?
   you have medicine protect vomit

water	naam duhhm	ນ້ຳດື່ມ
tissue	tiis'suu	ທິສຊູ
plastic bag	thong yaang	ຖົງຢາງ (slang for condom)

2) (Please) <u>stop</u> here.
   <u>Jawwt</u> bawn nii (daae).
   ຈອດບ່ອນນີ້ (ແຕ່)
   stop here please

3) I <u>need</u> to use the toilet. Now!
   Khawy <u>dtawng'gan</u> hawng naam. Di'ow nii!
   ຂ້ອຍຕ້ອງການຫ້ອງນ້ຳ. ດຽວນີ້!
   I need to in toilet. Now

4) Where is the emergency <u>exit</u>?
   <u>Ba'dtuu</u> suk'suhhn yuu saii?
   ປະຕູສຸກເສີນຢູ່ໃສ?
   door exit at where

5) Is the driver <u>sleepy</u>?
   Kon khap baw <u>nguang nawn</u> baww?
   ຄົນຂັບບໍ່ງ່ວງນອນບໍ່?
   person drive sleepy

6) Does this <u>bus</u> have brakes?
   <u>Lot'meh</u> kan'nii mii bay baww?
   ລົດເມຄັນນີ້ມີເບກບໍ່?
   bus this have brakes

47

Are we there yet?

1) Can I sit <u>here/on the roof</u>?
   Khawy khaww nang <u>yuu nii/tuhng lang'kaa</u> daii baww?
   ຂ້ອຍຂໍນັ່ງ ຢູ່ນີ້/ເທິງຫຼັງຄາ ໄດ້ບໍ?
   I may sit at here/on roof can

2) How long will <u>we</u> be here?
   <u>Pu'ak'how</u> ja yuu nii iik don paan daii?
   ພວກເຮົາຈະຢູ່ນີ້ອີກດົນປານໃດ?
   we will at more how long

3) Are you going to <u>Vang Viang</u>?
   Jow ja paii <u>Wang Wiang</u> baww?
   ເຈົ້າຈະໄປວັງວຽງບໍ?
   you will go Vang Viang

4) Can you give me a ride?
   Jow paii song khawy daii baww?
   ເຈົ້າໄປສົ່ງຂ້ອຍໄດ້ບໍ?
   you go send I can

5) Wait a minute.
   Thaa jak'nawy/thaa'buht'nuhng.
   ຖ້າຈັກໜ່ອຍ/ຖ້າບຶດໜຶ່ງ
   wait a little/wait moment one

VII. Getting Around Town

1) Where are you going?
   Jow (ja/si) paii saii?
   ເຈົ້າ (ຈະ/ຊິ) ໄປ ໃສ?
   you (will) go where?

2) I'd like to go to the/a .....
   Khawy yaak paii .....
   ຂ້ອຍຢາກໄປ .....
   I want to go .....

   Sentences are often started with just paii.

   To the .....   paii .....   ໄປ .....

   Question sentences are simple: Object + Question Word.

   Where is the............?
   ....yuu saii?
   ....ຢູ່ໃສ?
   ....at where?

airport	sa'naam bin	ສະໜາມບິນ
vank	ta'naa'kaan	ທະນາຄານ
border	khawp khayt, saai daaen	ຂອບເຂດ, ຊາຍແດນ
embassy	sa'thaan tuut	ສຖານທູດ + country
evening market	dta'laat laaeng	ຕະຫຼາດແລງ
fountain	naam pu	ນ້ຳພຸ
Friendship Bridge	khuua mit'dta'paap	ຂົວມິດຕະພາບ
immigration	gom gu'at kon khow muhh'ang	ກົມກວດຄົນເຂົ້າເມືອງ
internet	in'dterr'net	ອິນເຕີເນັດ
mekong	maae naam khawng	ແມ່ນ້ຳຂອງ
monument	aa'nu saa'wa'lii	ອານຸສາວະລີ
morning market	ata'laat'sao	ຕະຫຼາດເຊົ້າ
pharmacy	haan khaai yaa	ຮ້ານຂາຍຢາ
police station	sa'thaa'nii dtaam lu'at	ສະຖານີຕຳຫຼວດ
post office	hawng gaan paii' sa' nii	ຫ້ອງການໄປສະນີ
telecom center	suun too' la'sap	ສູນໂທລະສັບ
temple	wat	ວັດ
this address	tii yuu dtoo nii	ທີ່ຢູ່ໂຕນີ້
travel agency	baww'li'sat tawng ti'ow	ບໍລິສັດທ່ອງທ່ຽວ

Getting a Reasonable Price

1) How much?
   Tow daii?
   ເທົ່າໃດ

2) How much per person?
   Laa'kaa tow daii dtaww phuu nuhng?
   ລາຄາເທົ່າໃດຕ່ອຜູ້ໜຶ່ງ?
   price how much per person one

50

3) That's <u>too</u> expensive.

    Paaeng <u>poot.</u>

    ແພງໂພດ

    expensive too

    No, (it's) not expensive.

    Baww, (man) baw paaeng.

    ບໍ່, (ມັນ) ບໍ່ແພງ

    no, it no expensive

4) (It's) <u>very far.</u>

    (Man) <u>gaii laai.</u>

    (ມັນ) ໄກຫຼາຍ

    far very

(Use your hands: near, far and chicken sound very similar)

    (It's) not far. It's close.

    (Man) baw gaii. Yuu gaii gaii nii.

    ມັນບໍ່ໄກ ຢູ່ໃກ້ໆນີ້

5) Can I have a discount?

    Lut daii baww?

    ຫຼຸດໄດ້ບໍ່?

    discount can

Instructions

1) Turn <u>left/right.</u>
   Li'ow <u>saai/khuaa.</u>
   ລ້ຽວ ຊ້າຍ/ຂວາ
   turn left/right

2) Go straight.
   Paii suhh'suhh.
   ໄປຊື່ໆ
   go straight

3) You passed it.
   Jow gaai maa laae'o.
   ເຈ້ົາກາຍມາແລ້ວ
   you passed come already

4) Turn around.
   Gap kuhhn.
   ກັບຄືນ

5) Stop here.
   Jawt nii.
   ຈອດນີ້
   stop this

6) Careful!
   La wang.
   ລະວັງ

7) Can you <u>slow down</u>?
   Jow khap <u>saa'saa</u> daii baww?
   ເຈ້ົາຂັບຊ້າໆ ໄດ້ບໍ່?
   you drive slow can

8) Can you go <u>faster</u>?

Jow khap <u>wai'wai</u> daii baww?

ເຈົ້າຂັບໄວໆ ໄດ້ບໍ?

you drive fast can

Random Questions

1) How fast does this <u>tuk-tuk</u> go?

<u>Dtuk dtuk</u> pai wai'sut daii tao daii?

ຕຸກໆ ໄປໄວສຸດໄດ້ເທົ່າໃດ?

dtuk dtuk go fast–est how much

2) You're the best driver in the <u>city/Vientiane.</u>

Jow khap lot dii laai tii'sut naii <u>muhh'ang nii/Vientiane.</u>

ເຈົ້າຂັບລົດດີຫຼາຍທີ່ສຸດໃນເມືອງນີ້ / ວຽງຈັນ

you drive car good very best in city this/Vientiane

3) May I <u>drive</u>?

Khawy khaww <u>khap</u> daii baww?

ຂ້ອຍຂໍຂັບໄດ້ບໍ?

I may drive can

4) Do you have <u>change</u>?

Jow mii <u>ng´n pian</u> baww?

ເຈົ້າມີເງິນປ່ຽນບໍ?

you have change

5) Do you speak <u>English</u>?

Jow wow paasaa <u>ang'git</u> daii baww?

ເຈົ້າເວົ້າພາສາອັງກິດໄດ້ບໍ?

you speak language English can

VIII. Rentals & Repairs

1) Can I rent a ..... ?
   Khawy sao ..... daii baww?
   ຂ້ອຍເຊົ່າ ..... ໄດ້ບໍ?
   I rent ..... OK

bike	lot thiip	ລົດຖີບ
motorbike	lot jak	ລົດຈັກ
car	lot nyaii	ລົດໃຫຍ່
inner tube	gong yaang	ກົງຢາງ

2) How much per <u>hour/day/week</u>?
   Laa'kaa tao daii dtaww <u>su'aa moong/muhh/aa'tit</u> ?
   ລາຄາເທົ່າໃດຕໍ່ ຊົ່ວໂມງ/ມື້/ອາທິດ?
   price how much per hour/day/week

3) Do you have a <u>helmet/lock</u>?
   Jow mii <u>muak gan nawk/lawk</u> baww?
   ເຈົ້າມີ ໝວກກັນນ່ອກ/ລ່ອກ ບໍ?
   you have helmet/lock

4) I have a flat tire.
   Yaang lot khawy huua.
   ຢາງລົດຂ້ອຍຣົ່ວ
   rubber car I flat

5) Can you <u>fix</u> it?
> Jow <u>paaeng</u> daii baww?
> ເຈົ້າແປງໄດ້ບໍ?
> you fix able

6) Do you have a spark plug <u>key</u>?
> Jow mii <u>ga'jaae</u> khaii huaa'tian lot baww?
> ເຈົ້າມີກະແຈໄຂຫົວທຽນລົດບໍ?
> you have key open spark plug car

7) Please <u>fill</u> it up.
> Saii <u>dtem</u> thang.
> ໃສ່ເຕັມຖັງ

Instead of asking to fill the tank, it is common to tell the gas attendent how much you want to pay. For example: 5,000 Kip (Haa pan). In Laos, you do not pump your own gas.

IX. Just Plain lost

1) Where am I? = What <u>area/village</u> is this?
   Thaaeo/baan nii maaen baan nyang?
   ແຖວ/ບ້ານ ນີ້ແມ່ນບ້ານຫຍັງ?
   area/village this is village what

2) What <u>street</u> is this?
   Nii maaen tha'non nyang?
   ນີ້ແມ່ນຖະໜົນເສັ້ນໃດ?
   this is street what

3) I'm lost.
   Khawy long'taang.
   ຂ້ອຍຫຼົງທາງ
   I lost

4) I'm looking for .....
   Khawy (gam'lang) sawk'haa .....
   ຂ້ອຍ (ກຳລັງ) ຊອກຫາ .....
   I (–ing) look for .....

5) Where is ..... ?
   .... yuu saii?
   ..... ຢູ່ໃສ?
   ..... at where

Over there.
> yuu nan
> ຢູ່ນັ້ນ
> at there

North, east, south and west are not commonly used in Lao, but they are listed in the dictionary just in case.

X. Ordering Food & Drink

1) Do you have ..... ?
> Jow mii ..... baww?
> ເຈົ້າມີ ..... ບໍ່?
> you have .....

One bottle of <u>Beer Lao</u>, (please).
> Ow <u>Biaa Laao</u> gaaew nuhng (daae).
> ເອົາເບຍລາວແກ້ວໜຶ່ງ (ແດ່)
> take beer lao bottle one (please)

How much is a <u>beer</u>?
> <u>Biaa</u> laa'kaa tao daii?
> ເບຍລາຄາເທົ່າໃດ?
> beer price how much

2) With (out) .....
> (Baw) saii .....
> (ບໍ່) ໃສ່ .....
> (no) with ....

3) To go, please. (Take in a bag)
> Saii thong.
> ໃສ່ຖົງ
> with bag

4) <u>The check</u> please.

    <u>Gep ng'n/Sek bin</u> daae.

    ເກັບເງິນ/ເຊັກບິນ ແດ່

    check please

Meats & Fish

beef	siin ngu'ua	ຊີ້ນງົວ
chicken	gaii	ໄກ່
duck	pet	ເປັດ
fish	paa	ປາ
frog	gop	ກົບ
pork	muu	ໝູ
processed meat	luuk sin	ລູກສີນ
shrimp	gung	ກຸ້ງ
squid	paa'muhk	ປາໝຶກ
blood	luhh'at	ເລືອດ
egg	khaii	ໄຂ່
liver	dtap	ຕັບ
tofu	dtow huu	ເຕົາຮູ້

• Some soups come with liver and blood tofu, so it might be best to learn the simple phrase "Baw saii dtap, Baw saii luhh'at" (without liver, without blood) if these do not suit your fancy.

• You may come across a Lao delicacy called 'egg child' (ໄຂ່ລູກ) (khai lunk). It is a small egg. However, inside lies a little bird fetus.

• Another dish to be on the lockout for is called 'horse urine eggs' (ໄຂ່ຍ່ຽວມ້າ) (khai yiaow maa). The brownish—black, transparent eggs are fermented in horse urine.

Extras

bread	khow jii	ເຂົ້າຈີ່
chillies	maak phet	ໝາກເຜັດ
fish paste	ga'bi	ກະປີ
fish sauce	paa daaek	ປາແດກ
pepper	pik taii	ພິກໄທ
steamed rice	khow jow	ເຂົ້າຈ້າວ
processed pork	yaww	ຢໍ
salt	guhh'a	ເກືອ
sticky rice	khow ni'ow	ເຂົ້າໜຽວ
sugar	naam dtaan	ນ້ຳຕານ
sweet milk	nom khun	ນົມຂຸ້ນ
vinegar	naam som	ນ້ຳສົ້ມ

Note: "naam som" (vinegar) also refers to orange juice in Thai and is becoming a popular slang in Laos. Also, any snacks like crackers or bread are called khow nom (ເຂົ້າໜົມ).

XI. Most Common Lao Food

Soups

wet noodle	khow biak	ເຂົ້າປຽກ
thin noodle	ferr	ເຝີ
yellow noodle	mii luhh'ang	ໝີ່ເຫຼືອງ
tom yam	dtom nyam	ຕົ້ມຍຳ

Dishes

dry noodle in sauce	mii gawp	ໝີ່ກອບ
sour pork/ rice	naaem	ແໜມ
minced chicken/pork	laap gaii/muu	ລາບໄກ່/ໝູ
fried fish/chicken	juhhn baa/gaii	ຈືນ ປາ/ໄກ່
papaya salad	dtaam maak hung	ຕຳໝາກຮຸ່ງ
spring roll (soft, fried)	yaww khow, yaww juhhn	ຍໍຂາວ, ຍໍຈືນ

Sandwiches are sold out of shops and wheeled carts on almost every street corner in Vientiane. Choose the bread size and the vendor will fill it with cucumber, lettuce, tomato, yaww (processed pork), and a variety of sauces. If you want it with everything just say *so: "tuk sing tuk yaang"* or nod yes or no and say *"sai"* (with) or *"baw sai"* (without) as s(he) reaches for each topping.

Items

(One more) ..... please.
Ow ..... (iik an'nuhng) daae.
ເອົາ ..... (ອີກອັນໜຶ່ງ) ແດ່
take ..... more one please

bowl	thu'ai	ຖ້ວຍ
chopsticks	maii thuu	ໄມ້ຖູ່
fork	sawm	ສ້ອມ
glass	jawwk	ຈອກ
ice	naam gawn	ນ້ຳກ້ອນ
knife	miit	ມີດ
plate	jaan	ຈານ
spoon	buang	ບວງ
tissue (napkin)	ga'daat, tiis'suu	ກະດາດ, ທິສຊູ
toothpick	mai jiim khaae'o	ໄມ້ຈີ້ມແຂ້ວ

Fruits & Veggies

fruit	maak maii	ໝາກໄມ້
vegetables	phak	ຜັກ

apple	maak aep'buhhn	ໝາກແອັບເປີ້ນ
banana	maak gu'ai	ໝາກກ້ວຍ
cabbage	ga laam	ກະລ່ຳ
coconut	maak pown	ໝາກພ້າວ
corn	maak sa'lii	ໝາກສະລີ
cucumber	maak dtaaeng	ໝາກແຕງ
durian	maak tu'lian	ໝາກທຸລຽນ
dragon fruit	maak mang gawn	ໝາກມັງກອນ
jack fruit	maak mii	ໝາກມີ້
lettuce	phak sa'lat	ຜັກສະຫຼັດ

lime	maak noww	ໝາກນາວ
lychee	maak liin'jii	ໝາກລິ້ນຈີ່
mango	maak muang	ໝາກມ່ວງ
mangosteen	maak mang kut	ໝາກມັງຄຸດ
melon	maak dtaaeng nyaii	ໝາກແຕງໃຫຍ່
mint	phak hawm laai	ຜັກຫອມລາບ
mushroom	het	ເຫັດ
onion	phat buaa nyaii	ຜັກບົ່ວໃຫຍ່
orange	maak giang	ໝາກກ້ຽງ
papaya	maak hung	ໝາກຮຸ່ງ
peanuts	maak thuua din	ໝາກຖົ່ວດິນ
pear	maak saa'sii	ໝາກສາລີ້
pineapple	maak nat	ໝາກນັດ
potato*	man fha'lang	ມັນຝະລັ່ງ
pumpkin	maak uh	ໝາກອຶ
rambuttan	maak ngaw	ໝາກເງາະ
spring onion	phak buua baii	ຜັກບົ່ວໃບ
sprouts	maak thuua ngawk	ໝາກຖົ່ວງອກ
tomato	maak len	ໝາກເລັ່ນ
watermelon	maak moo	ໝາກໂມ

* Note: "man fhalang" is sometimes used as a word play on fhalang (foreigner).

XII. Beer Lao

Do you have a <u>bottle opener</u>?
Jow mii <u>khawng buhht gaae'o</u> baww?
ເຈົ້າມີຂອງເປີດແກ້ວບໍ່?
you have thing open bottle?

drink

beer Lao	biaa Laao	ເບຍລາວ
coffee	gaa'fhay	ກາເຟ
coke	kook	ໂຄກ
fruit shake	naam maak......pan	ນ້ຳໝາກ.....ປັ່ນ
combo	naam maak......pan gap maak....pan pon gan	
	ນ້ຳໝາກ.....ປັ່ນກັບໝາກ.....ປັ່ນປົນກັນ	

fresh Milk	nom sot	ນົມສົດ
Mirinda	mi'lin'daa	ມິລິນດາ
Ovaltine	oo'wan' dtiin	ໂອວັນຕິນ
Pepsi	pep'sii	ເປັບຊີ
7Up	sayi'wen'ap	ເຊເວັນອັບ
soy milk	naam dtow huu	ນ້ຳເຕົ້າຮູ້
sugarcane	naam aawi	ນ້ຳອ້ອຍ
tea (hot, cold)	naam saa (hawn, yen)	ນ້ຳຊາ (ຮ້ອນ, ເຢັນ)
water	naam duhhm	ນ້ຳດື່ມ
whiskey	Laao	ເຫຼົ້າ

XIII. For Smokers

ashtray	naae'o khiaa khii	ແຄນວດຄອຍຂີ້
pipe	gawk yaa	ກາກຢາ
cigarettes	yaa suup	ຢາສູບ
lighter	gap fhaii	ກັບໄຟ
matches	maii khiit fhaii	ໄມ້ຂີດໄຟ
papers	dtap dtawng	ຕັບຕ້ອງ
tobacco	yaa sen	ຢາເສັ້ນ

1) Do you smoke?
   Jow suup yaa baww?
   ເຈົ້າສູບຢາບໍ່?
   you smoke medicine

2) Would you like a <u>cigarette</u>?
   Jow yaak <u>suup yaa</u> baww?
   ເຈົ້າຢາກສູບຢາບໍ່?
   you want smoke medicine

3) Can I have a <u>cigarette</u>?
   Khaww <u>yaa suup</u> daii baww?
   ຂໍຢາສູບໄດ້ບໍ່?
   please medicine smoke can

4) Do you have <u>matches</u>?
   Jow mii <u>maii khiit fhaii</u> baww?
   ເຈົ້າມີ<u>ໄມ້ຂີດໄຟ</u>ບໍ່?
   you have matches

5) Can I borrow your <u>lighter</u>?
   Khaww yuhhm <u>gap fhaii</u> daii baww?
   ຂໍຢືມ<u>ກັບໄຟ</u>ໄດ້ບໍ່?
   please borrow lighter can

6) Can I smoke <u>here</u>?
   Khawy suup yaa <u>yuu nii</u> daii baww?
   ຂ້ອຍສູບຢາ<u>ຢູ່ນີ້</u>ໄດ້ບໍ່?
   Is moke medicine at this can

xiv. Out On the Town

1) What's your name?
   Jow suhh nyang?
   ເຈົ້າຊື່ຫຍັງ?
   you name what

2) Would you like to <u>dance</u> (with me)?
   Khawy khaw <u>dten</u> gap jow daii baww?
   ຂ້ອຍຂໍເຕັ້ນກັບເຈົ້າໄດ້ບໍ່?
   I may dance with you can

3) Can you teach me to <u>dance</u>?
   Jow sawn khawy <u>dten</u> daae daii baww?
   ເຈົ້າສອນຂ້ອຍເຕັ້ນແດ່ໄດ້ບໍ່?
   you teach me dance please can

4) I can't hear you.
   Khawy baw daii nyin jow.
   ຂ້ອຍບໍ່ໄດ້ຍິນເຈົ້າ
   I no can hear you

5) It's too <u>loud</u>.
   Siang <u>dang</u> poot.
   ຊຽງດັງໂພດ
   sound loud too

6) What?
   Maaen'nyang?
   ແມ່ນຫຍັງ?

7) What are you <u>doing</u>?
   Jow <u>het</u> nyang yuu?
   ເຈົ້າ<u>ເຮັດ</u>ຫຍັງຢູ່?
   you do what here

8) I'm waiting for a <u>friend</u>.
   Khawy (gam lang) thaa <u>muu</u>.
   ຂ້ອຍ (ກຳລັງ) ຖ້າ<u>ຫມູ່</u>
   I (ing) wait friend

9) Can I borrow your <u>pen</u>?
   Khawy khaww yuhhm <u>bik</u> daii baww?
   ຂ້ອຍຂໍຢືມ<u>ບິກ</u>ໄດ້ບໍ່?
   I may borrow pen can?

10) Wait a minute.
   Thaa buht nuhng/Jak nawy.
   ຖ້າບຶດຫນື່ງ/ຈັກຫນ້ອຍ
   wait moment one/how many little

11) Can I leave my <u>bike</u> here?
   (and will you keep and eye on it)?
   Khawy fhaak <u>lot</u> daii baww?
   ຂ້ອຍຝາກ<u>ລົດ</u>ໄດ້ບໍ່?
   I leave bike can

XV. Shopping

1) I'm looking for <u>soap</u>.
   Khawy sawk'haa <u>sa'buu.</u>
   ຂ້ອຍຊອກຫາສະບູ
   I look for soap

2) Do you have <u>shampoo</u>?
   Jow mii <u>yaa sa'phom/sam'puu</u> baww?
   ເຈົ້າມີຢາສະຜົມ/ແຊມພູບໍ?
   you have <u>medicine wash hair/ shampoo</u>

3) What material is this?
   An'nii het jaak nyang?
   ອັນນີ້ເຮັດຈາກຫຍັງ?
   thing this make from what

4) Do you have this in <u>black</u>?
   Jow mii an'nii <u>sii daam</u> baww?
   ເຈົ້າມີອັນນີ້ສີດຳບໍ?
   you have thing this color black

5) Do you have this any <u>smaller/larger</u>?
   Jow mii an'nii <u>nawy/nyai</u> guaa baww?
   ເຈົ້າມີອັນນີ້ ນ້ອຍ/ໃຫຍ່ ກວ່າບໍ?
   you have thing this bigger/smaller

6) Do you have any <u>other ones/colors</u>?

Jow mii <u>baaep uhhn/sii uhhn</u> iik baww?

ເຈົ້າມີ <u>ແບບອື່ນ/ສີອື່ນ</u> ອີກບໍ?

you have other ones/colors more

7) Can I <u>try</u> this <u>on</u>?

Khawy <u>lawng</u> daii baww?

ຂ້ອຍ<u>ລອງ</u>ໄດ້ບໍ?

I try on can

8) It's too <u>tight/ loose</u>.

<u>kap/lom</u> poot.

<u>ຄັບ/ຫຼົມ</u> ໂພດ

tight/ loose too

9) It's too <u>long/short.</u>

<u>nyow/san</u> poot.

<u>ຍາວ/ສັ້ນ</u> ໂພດ

long/ short too

10) Can you <u>alter/fix</u> this?

Jow dtat <u>awwk/paaeng</u> bawn nii daii baw?

ເຈົ້າຕັດ <u>ອອກ/ແປງ</u> ບ່ອນນີ້ໄດ້ບໍ?

you alter/ fix spot this can?

11) Can you make a <u>Lao dress</u> for me?

Jow dtat <u>sin</u> haii khawy daii baww?

ເຈົ້າຕັດສິ້ນໃຫ້ຂ້ອຍໄດ້ບໍ

you cut Lao dress give me can

12) Can I have a <u>receipt</u>?

Khaww <u>bin</u> daae?

ຂໍບິນແດ່?

may receipt please

13) Do you have a <u>bag</u>?

> Jow mii <u>thong</u> baww?
>
> ເຈົ້າມີຖົງບໍ?
>
> you have bag

14) What time do you <u>open/close</u>?

> <u>Buhht/Bit</u> jak moong?
>
> ເປີດ/ປິດ ຈັກໂມງ?
>
> open/ close what time

XVI. Clothes & Jewelry

backpack	ga'bow pay	ກະເປົາເປ້
bag	thong	ຖົງ
belt	saai aae'o	ສາຍແອວ
blanket	phaa hom	ຜ້າຮົ່ມ
bra	suhh'a sawn	ເສື້ອຊ້ອນ
bracelet	pa lak khaaen	ປະຫຼັກແຂນ
dress	ga poong	ກະໂປ່ງ
long dress	ga poong pen sut	ກະໂປ່ງເປັນຊຸດ
earrings	dtum huu	ຕຸ້ມຫູ
hat	muak	ໝວກ
jacket	suhh'a kum	ເສື້ອຄຸມ
jewelry	kuhh'ang pet, pawy	ເຄື່ອງເພັດ, ພອຍ
Lao skirt	sin	ສິ້ນ
Lao shirt	sut pa'jaam saat laao	ຊຸດປະຈຳຊາດລາວ
long-sleeved	khaaen nyow	ແຂນຍາວ
necklace	saai kaww	ສາຍຄໍ
pants	soong	ໂສ້ງ
raincoat	suhh'a gan fhon	ເສື້ອກັນຝົນ
ring	waaen	ແຫວນ
sandals	guhhp dtae	ເກີບແຕະ
scarf	phaa pan kaww	ຜ້າພັນຄໍ
shoes	guhhp	ເກີບ
shirt (T)	suhh'a	ເສື້ອ
short-sleeves	suhh'a khaaen san	ເສື້ອແຂນສັ້ນ
socks	thong dtiin	ຖົງຕີນ

sunglasses	waaen dtaa gan daaet	ແວ່ນຕາກັນແດດ
tie	gaa la wat	ກາລະວັດ
underwear	sa lip	ສະຫຼິບ
umbrella	kan hom	ຄັນຮົ່ມ
wallet	ga'bow ng´n	ກະເປົາເງິນ
zipper	sip	ຊິບ

Colors

red	sii daaeng	ສີແດງ
orange	sii naam maak giang	ສີນ້ຳໝາກກ້ຽງ
yellow	sii luhh'ang	ສີເຫລືອງ
green	sii khi'ow	ສີຂຽວ
blue	sii fhaa	ສີຟ້າ
pink	sii bu'aa	ສີບົວ
purple	sii muang	ສີມ່ວງ
white	sii khaow	ສີຂາວ
black	sii daam	ສີດຳ
brown	sii naam dtaan	ສີນ້ຳຕານ
gray	sii khuhh thow	ສີຂີ້ເຖົ້າ
dark blue	sii fhaa khem	ສີຟ້າເຂັ້ມ
light red	sii daaeng jaaet	ສີແດງແຈດ

Material

aluminum	aa'luu mii'niam	ອະລູມີນຽມ
bone	ga duuk	ກະດູກ
brass	tawng luhh'ang	ທອງເຫຼືອງ
bronze	tawng saam'lit	ທອງສຳລິດ
cloth	phaa	ຜ້າ
copper	tawng daaeng	ທອງແດງ
cotton	fhaai	ຝ້າຍ
gold	kaam	ຄຳ

leather	nang	ໜັງ
linen	phaa li'nin	ผ้าลิมิม
rayon	phaa ni long	ผ้ามิลัງ
silk	maii	ไໝม
silver	ng´n	ເງິນ
teak	mai sak	ไม้สัก
wood	maii	ไม้
wool	khon gae	ຂົນແກະ

STONES

diamond	pet	ເພັກ
emerald	maw'la'got	ມໍລະກົດ
gems	pawy	ພອຍ
jade	yok	ຍົກ
ruby	tap tim	ທັບທິມ
sapphire	pawy lii kaam	ພອຍສີຄາມ

XVII. At the Hairdresser

1) How much is a haircut/manicure/pedicure?
   Dtat phom/het lep muhh/het lep dtiin tao daii?
   ຕັດຜົມ/ເຮັດເລັບມື/ເຮັດເລັບຕີນ ເທົ່າໃດ?
   haircut/ manicure/ pedicure how much

2) Can you <u>wash</u> and <u>massage</u> my hair?
   <u>Sa</u> laae <u>nu'at</u> phom haii khawy daii baww?
   <u>ສະ</u>ແລະ<u>ນວດ</u>ຜົມໃຫ້ຂ້ອຍໄດ້ບໍ່?
   wash and massage hair give me can

3) Don't use <u>shampoo/conditioner</u>.
   Baw saii <u>yaa sa phom/kiim nuat phom.</u>
   ບໍ່ໃສ່ <u>ຢາສະຜົມ/ຄີມນວດຜົມ</u>
   no use shampoo / conditioner

4) Cut it short <u>on top/on the sides/in the back</u>.
   Dtat haii sanlong <u>taang tuhngtaang khaang/ taang lang.</u>
   ຕັດໃຫ້ສັ້ນລົງ <u>ທາງເທິງ / ທາງຂ້າງ / ທາງຫຼັງ</u>
   cut give short(er) way top/way side/way back

5) I like it long.
   Khawy mak haii man nyow.
   ຂ້ອຍມັກໃຫ້ມັນຍາວ
   I like give it long

75

6) Use the <u>electric razor/scissors.</u>
   Saii <u>dtawng derr thaae/miit dtat.</u>
   ໃຊ້ຕ່ອງເດີແຮງ/ມີດຕັດ
   use electric razor/scissors

7) Can you blow-dry my hair?
   Daii phom haii daae.
   ໃດຜົມໃຫ້ແດ່
   dry hair give please

8) Do you have <u>gel / hair spray</u>?
   Mii <u>yay'o / sa'pay</u> baww?
   ມີ ເຢໂອ / ສະເປ ຜົມບໍ່?
   have gel / spray hair

9) Do you have a <u>mirror</u>?
   Mii <u>waaen'nyaaeng</u> baww?
   ມີແຄ່ນແຍງບໍ່?
   have mirror

10) That hurts.
    Jep.
    ເຈັບ

11) That feels good.
    Huu'suhhk kak laai.
    ຮູ້ສຶກຄັກຫຼາຍ
    feel good very

12) The water is too hot/ cold.
    Naam <u>hawn/yen</u> poot.
    ນ້ຳ ຮ້ອນ/ເຢັນ ໂພດ
    water hot/cold too

76

13) It looks good.

    Kak laai, Ngaam laai.

    ຄັກຫຼາຍ, ງາມຫຼາຍ

    good very, pretty very

XVIII. Photography

1) How much is it to develop film?
   Kaa'laang huup tao daii?
   ຄ່າລ້າງຮູບເທົ່າໃດ?
   price develop photo how much

2) B&W/Color film
   Fim khow daam/Fim sii
   ຟິມຂາວດຳ/ຟິມສີ
   film white black/film color

3) Slides
   sa'lai
   ສະໄລ້

4) <u>24 / 36</u> exposures
   <u>saao sii / saam sip hok</u> poo
   <u>ຊາວສີ / ສາມສິບຫົກ</u> ໂປ້
   24 / 36 exposures

5) Do you develop <u>slides</u>?
   <u>Saai sa'laii</u> daii baww?
   <u>ສາຍສະໄລ້</u>ໄດ້ບໍ?
   slide can

6) Can you print the white borders?
   Jow at huup saii khawp khow daii baww?
   ເຈົ້າອັດຮູບໃສ່ຂອບຂາວໄດ້ບໍ?
   you print photo put border white can

7) How much is the processing fee?
   Kaa at huup tao daii?
   ຄ່າອັດຮູບເທົ່າໃດ?
   price print photo how much

8) How much per print/reprints?
   At phaaen la tao daii?
   ອັດແຜ່ນລະເທົ່າໃດ?
   print piece each how much

9) Can I have a discount if I develop ..... rolls?
   Jow lut daii baw thaa khawy laang ..... muu'an?
   ເຈົ້າຫຼຸດໄດ້ບໍ່ຖ້າຂ້ອຍລ້າງ ..... ມ້ວນ?
   you discount can if I develop ..... roll

10) Can you develop this in an hour?
    Jow laan laae'o paai naii nuhng suua moong baww?
    ເຈົ້າລ້າງແລ້ວພາຍໃນໜຶ່ງຊົ່ວໂມງບໍ?
    you develop already in one hour

11) When will it be ready?
    Man ja laae'o jak moong?
    ມັນຈະແລ້ວຈັກໂມງ?
    It will ready what time

12) Can you print doubles?
    Laang naae'o la sawng baii daii baww?
    ລ້າງແນວລະສອງໃບໄດ້ບໍ?
    develop thing each 2 piece can

13) Can you fix my camera?

    Paaeng gawng thaai'huup daii baww?

    ແປງກ້ອງຖ່າຍຮູບໄດ້ບໍ?

    fix camera can

14) My camera won't rewind. Can you get the film out?

    Gawng thaai'huup khawy baw lii'waai. Ow fim awwk
    daae daii baww?

    ກ້ອງຖ່າຍຮູບຂ້ອຍບໍ່ລີ້ວາຍ. ເອົາຟີມອອກແດ່ໄດ້ບໍ

    camera I no rewind. Take film out please can

15) Do you have cleaning papers?

    Mii jiaa taam kuaam sa'aat baww?

    ມີເຈ້ຍທຳຄວາມສະອາດບໍ?

    have paper do clean can

16) Do you sell <u>cameras</u>?

    Mii <u>gawng thaai'huup</u> khow baww?

    ມີ<u>ກ້ອງຖ່າຍຮູບ</u>ຂາຍບໍ?

    have camera sell?

xix. Time?

1) What time is it?

Jak <u>moong</u> laaeo?

ຈັກ<u>ໂມງ</u>ແລ້ວ?

what <u>o'clock</u> already

2) What day is it?

<u>Muhh'nii</u> maaen wan nyang?

ມື້ນີ້ແມ່ນວັນຫຍັງ?

<u>today</u> is day what

3) What's the date today?

Muhh'nii wan'tii tao daii?

ມື້ນີ້ວັນທີເທົ່າໃດ?

today date how much

4) <u>How long</u> have you been here?

Jow yuu nii <u>don</u> laae'o?

ເຈົ້າຢູ່ນີ້ດົນແລ້ວ?

you at this how long already

5) How long will you be <u>here</u>?

Jow ja <u>yuu nii</u> iik don daii?

ເຈົ້າຈະຢູ່ນີ້ອີກດົນໃດ?

you will at this more how long

6) When <u>will</u> it <u>leave</u>?

    Dtawn daii man ja <u>paii/awwk</u>?

    ຕອນໃດມັນຈະໄປ/ອອກ?

    when it will go/will out

7) When <u>will</u> it <u>arrive</u>?

    Dtawn daii man <u>ja maa hawt</u>?

    ຕອນໃດມັນຈະມາຮອດ?

    when it will come arrive

8) How long does it take?

    Saii way'laa don paan daii?

    ໃຊ້ເວລາດົນປານໃດ?

    use time how long can

9) Do you have any <u>time</u>?

    Jow mii <u>way'laa</u> iik baww?

    ເຈົ້າມີເວລາອີກບໍ່?

    you have time any more

10) I (don't) have <u>enough</u> time.

    Khawy mii way'laa (baw) <u>paww</u>.

    ຂ້ອຍມີເວລາ(ບໍ່)ພໍ

    I have time (not) enough

11) I (don't) have <u>time</u>.

    Khawy (baw) mii <u>way'laa</u>.

    ຂ້ອຍ(ບໍ່)ມີເວລາ

    I (no) have time

12) Are you <u>ready</u> yet?

    Jow <u>pawm</u> laae'o baww?

    ເຈົ້າພ້ອມແລ້ວບໍ່?

    you ready already

13) I'm finished/I'm done.

> Khawy laae'o laae'o.
>
> ຂ້ອຍແລ້ວໆ
>
> I already already

It's finished/It's empty.

> Mot laae'o.
>
> ໝົດແລ້ວ
>
> finished already

Real Time

1 hour(s)	nuhng su'aa moong	ໜຶ່ງຊົ່ວໂມງ
minute(s)	naa'tii	ນາທີ
time	way'laa	ເວລາ
2 o'clock	sawng moong	ສອງໂມງ

before	gawn	ກ່ອນ
early/ fast	wai	ໄວ
late	maa saa	ມາຊ້າ
later (after that)	lang jaak nan	ຫຼັງຈາກນັ້ນ
on Time	dtong way'laa	ຕົງເວລາ
slow	saa	ຊ້າ

1:00 am
nuhng moong <u>dtong (sao)</u>   ໜຶ່ງໂມງຕົງ (ເຊົ້າ)
2:00 pm
sawng moong <u>dtong (su'ai)</u>   ສອງໂມງຕົງ (ສວຍ)
12:00 noon
sip sawng moong/<u>tiang dtong</u>   ສິບສອງໂມງ/<u>ທຽງຕົງ</u>
12:00 midnight
sip sawng <u>moong dtong/tiang kuhhn</u>   ສິບສອງ ໂມງຕົງ/<u>ທຽງຄືນ</u>
4:30
sii moong k´ng   ສີໂມງເຄິ່ງ

Times of Day

morning	dtawnn sao	ຕອນເຊົ້າ
afternoon	dtawn su'ai	ຕອນສວຍ
evening	dtawn laaeng	ຕອນແລງ

day	muhh	ມື້
night	kh'uhhn	ຄືນ

last night	muh'kuhhn nii	ມື້ຄືນນີ້
today	muhh'nii	ມື້ນີ້
tomorrow	muhh'uhhn	ມື້ອື່ນ
tomorrow morning	muhh'uhhn sao	ມື້ອື່ນເຊົ້າ
tomorrow afternoon	muhh'uhhn dtawn su'ai	ມື້ອື່ນຕອນສວຍ
tomorrow evening	muhh'uhhn dtawn laaeng	ມື້ອື່ນຕອນແລງ
the day after tomorrow	muhh'huhh	ມື້ຮື
in 4 days	paai naii sii muhh	ພາຍໃນ 4 ມື້
next week	aa'tit naa	ອາທິດໜ້າ

yesterday	muhh waan'nii	ມື້ວານນີ້
the day before yesterday	muhh gawn'nii	ມື້ກ່ອນນີ້
3 days ago	saam muhh gawn	3ມື້ກ່ອນ

Frequency

always	luhh'ai luhh'ai	ເລື້ອຍໆ
usually	dtaam poka'dtii	ຕາມປົກກະຕິ
often	luhh'ai luhh'ai	ເລື້ອຍໆ
sometimes	bang way'laa	ບາງເວລາ
occasionally	bang kang kow	ບາງຄັ້ງຄາວ
never	baw kuhh'y	ບໍ່ເຄີຍ

Questionables

perhaps	aat'ja, baang tii	ວາດຈະ, ບາງທີ
maybe	baang tuhh'a	ບາງເທື່ອ
doubtfully	aat'ja baww	ອາດຈະບໍ່
no way	baw mii taang	ບໍ່ມີທາງ

Quantities

one <u>day</u>,	<u>muhh</u> nuhng	ມື້ອນນຶ່ງ
two days	sawng muhh	ສອງມື້
three days	saam muhh	ສາມມື້
<u>every</u>day	<u>tuk'tuk</u> muhh	ທຸກທຸກມື້
one <u>week</u>	<u>aa'tit</u> nuhng	ອາທິດນຶ່ງ
one <u>month</u>	<u>duhh'an</u> nuhng	ເດືອນນຶ່ງ
one <u>year</u>	<u>pii</u> nuhng	ປີນຶ່ງ

Days of the Week

Sunday	wan (aa)tit	ວັນ (ອາ) ທິດ
Monday	wan jan	ວັນຈັນ
Tuesday	wan (ang) kaan	ວັນ (ອັງ) ຄານ
Wednesday	wan put	ວັນພຸດ
Thursday	wan pa'hat	ວັນພະຫັດ
Friday	wan suk	ວັນສຸກ
Saturday	wan sao	ວັນເສົາ
Weekend	taai aa'tit/	ທ້າຍອາທິດ/
	wan sao wan tit	ວັນເສົາວັນທິດ

Months

January	mang gawn	ມັງກອນ
February	gum paa	ກຸມພາ
March	mi naa	ມີນາ
April	may saa	ເມສາ
May	puht sa paa	ພຶດສະພາ
June	mi thu naa	ມິຖຸນາ
July	gaww la got	ກໍລະກົດ
August	sing haa	ສິງຫາ
September	gan nyaa	ກັນຍາ
October	dtu laa	ຕຸລາ
November	pa jik	ພະຈິກ
December	han waa	ທັນວາ

Instead, you can just say *duhh'an* (month) before the number of the month: July, duhh'an jet (month 7). See numbers on p. 97.

Seasons

seasons	la'duu gaan	ລະດູການ
Spring	la'duu baan maii	ລະດູບານໃໝ່
Fall	la'duu bai maii lon	ລະດູໃບໄມ້ລົ່ນ
Summer	la'duu hawn	ລະດູຮ້ອນ
Winter	la'duu naao	ລະດູໜາວ
Dry season	la'duu laaeng	ລະດູແລ້ງ
Wet (Monsoon)	la'duu fon	ລະດູຝົນ

Weather

cloud	mayk	ເມກ
cloudy	mayk mawk	ເມກ ໝອກ
drizzle	fhon fhawy	ຝົນຝອຍ
drought	haaeng laaeng	ແຫ້ງແລ້ງ
earthquake	phaaen din waii	ແຜ່ນດິນໄຫວ
fire	faii	ໄຟ
flood	naam thu'am	ນ້ຳຖ້ວມ
fog	naam mawk	ນ້ຳໝອກ
foggy	dtem paiidu'ai mawk	ເຕັມໄປດ້ວຍໝອກ
full moon	duhh'an dtem du'ang	ເດືອນເຕັມດວງ
hail	maak hep	ໝາກເຫັບ
lightning	faa maaep	ຟ້າແມບ
moon	du'ang duhh'an	ດວງເດືອນ
rain	fhon	ຝົນ
snow	hii'ma	ຫິມະ
stars	doww	ດາວ
sun	dtaa wen	ຕາເວັນ
sunny	daaet sawng	ແດດສ່ອງ
sunrise	dtaa wen awwk	ຕາເວັນອອກ
sunset	dtaa wen dtok din	ຕາເວັນຕົກດິນ
thunder	faa hawng	ຟ້າຮ້ອງ
thunderstorm	pa nyu fhon	ພາຍຸຝົນ
typhoon	lom dtai'fhun	ລົມໄຕ່ຝຸນ
wind	lom	ລົມ

XX. In Sickness & Health

1) Do you <u>feel</u> OK?

   Jow <u>huu'suhk</u> dii baww?

   ເຈົ້າຮູ້ສຶກດີບໍ່?

   you feel good

2) I feel OK.

   Khawy huu'suhk <u>dii</u>. / Khawy <u>sa'baai dii</u>.

   ຂ້ອຍຮູ້ສຶກດີ / ຂ້ອຍສະບາຍດີ

   I feel good./ I (am) good

3) I feel <u>sick</u>.

   Khawy baw sa'baai./Khawy <u>pen khaii.</u>

   ຂ້ອຍບໍ່ສະບາຍ/ຂ້ອຍເປັນໄຂ້

   I no good/I feel sick

4) You <u>look</u> sick.

   Jow <u>buhng</u> kuhh pen khaii.

   ເຈົ້າເບິ່ງຄືເປັນໄຂ້

   you look like sick

5) Do you need some <u>help</u>?

   Jow dtawng gaan <u>kuaam su'ai luhh'a</u> baww?

   ເຈົ້າຕ້ອງການຄວາມຊ່ວຍເຫຼືອບໍ່?

   you need help

6) Can I help you?
   Khawy sua'i jow daii baww?
   ຂ້ອຍຊ່ວຍເຈົ້າໄດ້ບໍ?
   I help what you can

7) Where is the <u>toilet</u>?
   <u>Hawng Naam</u> yuu sai
   ຫ້ອງນ້ຳຢູ່ໃສ?
   toilet at where

hospital	hoong maww	ໂຮງໝໍ
pharmacy	haan khaai yaa	ຮ້ານຂາຍຢາ
clinic	kii'nik	ຄລີນິກ

ouch!

I (have) (a) .....
khawy .....
ຂ້ອຍ .....

headache	jep huu'a	ເຈັບຫົວ
stomachache	jep tawng	ເຈັບທ້ອງ
sore throat	jep kaww	ເຈັບຄໍ
toothache	jep khaae'o	ເຈັບແຂ້ວ
It hurts (here)	jep (yuu nii)	ເຈັບ (ຢູ່ນີ້)

Just Plain Sick

allergies	pen puum paae	ເປັນພູມແພ້
car sick	mao lot	ເມົາລົດ
chills	noww san	ໜາວສັ່ນ
cold	khaii hu'at	ໄຂ້ຫວັດ

cough	aii	ໄອ
cramps	pan	ປັ້ນ
diarrhea	thawk tawng	ทอกข้อງ
dizzy	win hu'aa	ວິນຫົວ
fever	pen khaii	ເປັນໄຂ້
runny nose	khii muu laii	ຂີ້ມູກໄຫຼ
vomiting	haak	ຮາກ
worms	maae thawng	ແມ່ທ້ອງ

Diseases & Disorders

Aids	look ayyt	ໂລກເອດ
Asthma	pen huhht	ເປັນຫຶດ
Cholera	look a'hi'waa	ໂລກອະຫິວາ
Dengue fever	khaii saa	ໄຂ້ຊ່າ
Dysentary	look tawng bit	ໂລກທ້ອງບິດ
Hepatitis A/B	dtap ak sayp	ຕັບອັກເສບ
Malaria	khaii nyung /	ໄຂ້ຍຸງ/ມາເລເລຍ
	maa'lay'liaa	
Rabies	pen waw	ເປັນວໍ້

Medicine

1) Do you have any <u>medicine</u>?
   Jow mii <u>yaa</u> baww?
   ເຈົ້າມີຢາບໍ່?
   you have medicine

2) How many <u>pills</u> do I take at a time?
   Khawy dtawng gin <u>yaa</u> tuhh'a la jak met?
   ຂ້ອຍຕ້ອງກິນຢາເທື່ອລະຈັກເມັດ?
   I have (to) eat medicine time each how much

3) <u>How many</u> times a day?

    <u>Jak tuhh'a</u> dtaww muhh nuhng?

    ຈັກເທື່ອຕໍ່ມື້ໜຶ່ງ?

    How many times per day one

The Extras

Aspirin	yaa dtaan suhh'a	ຢາຕ້ານເຊື້ອ
Bandage	pha pan paae	ຜ້າພັນແຜ
cold medicine	yaa gaae wat	ຢາແກ້ຫວັດ
cough medicine	yaa dii aii	ຢາດີໄອ
condom	thong yaang a'naa maii	ຖົງຢາງອະນາໄມ
ear drops	yaa yawt huu	ຢາຢອດຫູ
eye drops	yaa yawt dtaa	ຢາຢອດຕາ
Iodine	aii'oo'diin	ໄອໂອດິນ
medicine	yaa	ຢາ
sleeping medicine	yaa nawn lap	ຢານອນຫຼັບ
tampon/pad	phaa a'naa maii	ຜ້າອະນາໄມ
tape	sa'gawt dtit	ສະກ໋ອດຕິດ

Doctor Vocabulary

doctor	taan maww	ທ່ານໝໍ
injection	yaa sak	ຢາສັກ
temperature	u na puum	ອຸນະພູມ
pulse	siip pa jawn	ຊີບພະຈອນ
vaccination	gaan puk siip	ການປຸກຊີບ

Body Parts

ankle	khaww dtiin	ຂໍ້ຕີນ
arms	khaaen	ແຂນ
back	lang	ຫຼັງ
blood	luhh'at	ເລືອດ
breast	nom	ນົມ
buttocks	gon	ກົ້ນ
chest	ehk	ເອິກ
chin	kaang	ຄາງ
ears	huu	ຫູ
elbow	khaaen sawk	ແຂນສອກ
eyes	dtaa	ຕາ
finger	niu muhh	ນິ້ວມື
foot	dtiin	ຕີນ
hair	phom	ຜົມ
hand	muhh	ມື
head	hu'aa	ຫົວ
heal	hak saa, pin puaa	ຮັກສາ, ປິ່ນປົວ
hips	sa pook	ສະໂພກ
joints	khaww dtaww	ຂໍ້ຕໍ່
knee	hu'aa khow	ຫົວເຂົ່າ
legs	khaa	ຂາ
lips	sop	ສົບ
liver	dtap	ຕັບ
mouth	baak	ປາກ
nail	lep muhh	ເລັບມື
neck	kaww	ຄໍ
nose	dang	ດັງ
penis	haam	ຫຳ
shoulders	baa laii	ບ່າ ໄລ່
stomach	tawng	ທ້ອງ
teeth	khaae'o	ແຂ້ວ

throat	kaww hawy	ຄໍທອຍ
toes	niu dtiin	ນິ້ວ ຕີນ
tongue	liin	ລິ້ນ
vagina	hii	ຫີ
waist	ban aae'o	ບັ້ນແອວ
wrist	khaww muhh	ຂໍ້ມື

XXI. Distress

1) stop!   jawt/yut!   ຈອດ/ຍຸດ!
2) hurry!   waii waii!   ໄວໆ!
3) slow down!   saa long!   ຊ້າລົງ!
4) help!   su'ai!   ຊ່ວຍ!
5) watch out!   la wang!   ລະວັງ

6. Where is the toilet?
   Hawng Naam yuu saii?
   ຫ້ອງນ້ຳຢູ່ໃສ?
   toilet at where

7. Do you have any tissues?
   Jow mii tiis'suu baww?
   ເຈົ້າມີທິສຊູບໍ່
   you have tissue

plastic bag(s)   thong yaang   ຖົງຢາງ
medicine to prevent vomiting   yaa gan haak   ຢາກັນຮາກ

8. Please take me to the hospital.
   Galunaa ow khawy paii hoong maww daae.
   ກະລຸນາເອົາຂ້ອຍໄປໂຮງໝໍແດ່
   please take me go hospital please

94

9) I <u>lost</u> my passport.

Khawy <u>het</u> paas'paww <u>siaa</u>.

ຂ້ອຍ<u>ເຮັດ</u>ປາສປໍ<u>ເສຍ</u>

I do passport lost

10) Please call the <u>police</u>.

Galunaa too haa <u>dtam'luat</u> daae.

ກະລຸນາໂທຫາ<u>ຕຳຫຼວດ</u>ແດ່

please call police please

(Instead of trying to call the police, go there.)

11) Can I use your <u>phone</u>?!

Khaww saii <u>too'la'sap</u> jow daii baww?

ຂໍໃຊ້<u>ໂທລະສັບ</u>ເຈົ້າໄດ້ບໍ?

please use phone you can

12) Get out of my way!

Yaa khuaang taang!

ຢ່າຂວາງທາງ!

Don't block way

13) I can't walk.

Nyaang baw daii.

ຍ່າງບໍ່ໄດ້

walk no can

14) Someone stole my <u>wallet</u>!

Mii kon lak <u>ga'bow ng´n</u> khawy!

ມີຄົນລັກ<u>ກະເປົາເງິນ</u>ຂ້ອຍ!

have person steal wallet (of) me

15) I'm <u>lost</u>.

      Khawy <u>long taang</u>.

      ຂ້ອຍຫຼົງທາງ

      I lost way

16) Where is the <u>Australian</u> *Embassy*?

      Sa'thaan'tuut <u>o'sa'dtaa'lii</u> *yuu saii*?

      ສະຖານທູດອົສະຕາລີຢູ່ໃສ?

      embassy Australia at where?

XXII. Numbers

• 1 and 20 have irregular variations, but the rest never change.

0	suun	ສູນ	20	saao	ຊາວ
1	nuhng	ໜຶ່ງ	21	saao et	ຊາວເອັດ
2	sawng	ສອງ	22	saao sawng	ຊາວສອງ
3	saam	ສາມ	30	saam sip	ສາມສິບ
4	sii	ສີ່	31	saam sip et	ສາມສິບເອັດ
5	haa	ຫ້າ	32	saam sip sawng	ສາມສິບສອງ
6	hok	ຫົກ	40	sii sip	ສີ່ສິບ
7	jet	ເຈັດ	50	haa sip	ຫ້າສິບ
8	paaet	ແປດ	60	hok sip	ຫກສິບ
9	gao	ເກົ້າ	70	jet sip	ເຈັດສິບ
10	sip	ສິບ	80	paaet sip	ແປດສິບ
11	sip et	ສິບເອັດ	90	gao sip	ເກົ້າສິບ
12	sip sawng	ສິບສອງ	100	nuhng lawy	ໜຶ່ງຫ້ອຍ
			200	sawng lawy	ສອງຫ້ອຍ

1,000 and Up

• Only the number "nuhng" (1) can come before and after "pan" (1000).

1,000	(nuhng) pan/ pan nuhng	(ໜຶ່ງ) ພັນ/ພັນໜຶ່ງ
2,000	sawng pan	ສອງພັນ
10,000	sip pan/(nuhng) muhhn	ສິບພັນ/ໜຶ່ງໝື່ນ
100,000	(nuhng) saaen	(ໜຶ່ງ) ແສນ
1,000,000	(nuhng) laan	(ໜຶ່ງ) ລ້ານ

First to Last

first	tii nuhng	ທີ່ໜຶ່ງ
second	tii sawng	ທີ່ສອງ
third	tii saam	ທີ່ສາມ
fourth	tii sii	ທີ່ສີ່
last	sut taai	ສຸດທ້າຍ

Fractions

one-fourth	nuhng su'an sii	ໜຶ່ງສ່ວນສີ່
one-half	nuhng su'an sawng	ໜຶ່ງສ່ວນສອງ
three-fourths	saam su'an sii	ສາມສ່ວນສີ່

Weights and Measures

centimeter	sen	ເຊັນ
gram	glaam	ກຼາມ
heavy	man	ໜັກ
kilogram	gi'loo	ກິໂລ
kilomete	gi'loo'maaet	ກິໂລແມັດ
light (adj)	bao	ເບົາ
liter	lit	ລິດ
long	nyow	ຍາວ
measure	taaek	ແທກ
meter	maaet	ແມັດ
narrow	kaaep	ແຄບ
pint	kuhng lit	ເຄິ່ງລິດ
short	san	ສັ້ນ
weigh	nak	ໜັກ
weight	naam nak	ນ້ຳໜັກ
wide	guaang	ກວ້າງ

xxiii. Grammar

I	Khawy	ຂ້ອຍ
You	Jow	ເຈົ້າ
She	Laao	ລາວ
You (pl)	Pu'ak jow	ພວກເຈົ້າ
They	Pu'ak khow	ພວກເຂົາ
We	Pu'ak how	ພວກເຮົາ

• As subjects, all of the above are often unspoken.

Important words of grammar:

This	an'nii	ອັນນີ້
That	an'nan	ອັນນັ້ນ
Here	yuu'nii	ຢູ່ນີ້
There	yuu'nan	ຢູ່ນັ້ນ

There are many forms of 'yes'.

Jow is a polite form, good for any occasion, with anyone. Are you from Iceland? (maa jak Iceland baww?) Yes, I am. (Jow)

Daii is used instead of jow to show ability, for example: Can you? (daii baww?) Yes I can. (Daii).

Uhh is common between friends or people who are friendly toward each other.

Maaen laae'o means "that's right."

Doy and Doy kha'nawy are spoken to monks, high officials and sometimes to elders such as parents or older siblings.

YES: Jow, Uhh, Maaen laae'o, Doy, Doy kha'nawy
ເຈົ້າ, ເອີ, ແມ່ນແລ້ວ, ໂດຍ, ໂດຍຂະນ້ອຍ

There is only word for NO: Baww ບໍ່

Baw is a shorter sound at the beginning or middle of a sentence and makes a sentence negative:

I eat meat.
    Khawy gin siin.
    ຂ້ອຍກິນຊີ້ນ
    I eat meat.

I (don't) eat meat.
    Khawy (baw) gin siin.
    ຂ້ອຍ (ບໍ່) ກິນຊີ້ນ
    I (no) eat meat.

"Baww" is drawn out at the end of a sentence and turns a statement into a question. In this case "baww" also changes the hidden subject. (I and you)

I am hungry.
    Hiu Khow.
    ຫິວເຂົ້າ

Are you <u>hungry</u>?

<u>Hiu khow</u> **baww?**

ຫິວເຂົ້າບໍ່?

PLEASE — KHAWW ຂໍ

Please bring some water.

<u>Khaww</u> naam haii khawy daae.

ຂໍ ນ້ຳ ໃຫ້ ຂ້ອຍ ແດ່

may water give me please

ALREADY — LAAEO ແລ້ວ

Have you already eaten?

Jow gin <u>laaeo</u> baww?

ເຈົ້າ ກິນ ແລ້ວ ບໍ່?

You eat <u>already</u>

WILL (future) — SI or JA ຊິ or ຈະ

Where are you going?

Jow <u>si/ja</u> paii saii?

ເຈົ້າ ຊິ/ໄປ ໃສ?

You will go where

ING (now) — GAM LANG ກຳລັງ

Note: often used with "si" or "ja" above

What are you doing now?

Jow <u>gamlang</u> het nyang di'ow niii?

ເຈົ້າ ກຳລັງ ເຮັດ ຫຍັງ ດຽວ ນີ້?

you–<u>ing</u> do what right now

HAS/ HAVE (EVER) BEEN — KUHH'Y ເຄີຍ

Have you (ever) been to Luang Prabang?

Jow <u>kuhh'y</u> paii Lu'ang Pa'bang baww?

ເຈົ້າ ເຄີຍ ໄປ ຫຼວງພະບາງ ບໍ່?

You <u>have been</u> to Luang Prabang?

NOT YET — NYANG   ยัງ

I haven't eaten <u>yet</u>.
Khawy <u>nyang</u> baw daii gin khow.
ຂ້ອຍ ຍັງ ບໍ່ ໄດ້ ກິນ ເຂົ້າ
I still not (past) eat food

PAST TENSE — DAII   ໄດ້

I went to Vang Vieng yesterday.
Khawy <u>daii</u> paii Wang Wiang muhh'waan'nii.
ຂ້ອຍ ໄດ້ ໄປ ວັງວຽງ ມື້ ວານນີ້
I (past) go Vang Viang yesterday

WHO — MAAEN PHAII?   ແມ່ນ ໃผ

Who are you?
Jow <u>maaen phaii</u>?
ເຈົ້າ ແມ່ນ ໃผ?
You are *who*

WHAT — MAAEN NYANG?   ແມ່ນ ຫຍັງ

What is this?
An'nii <u>maaen nyang</u>?
ອັນນີ້ ແມ່ນ ຫຍັງ
This is <u>what</u>

WHERE — YUU SAII?   ຢູ່ ໃສ

Where is the toilet?
Hawng naam <u>yuu saii</u>?
ຫ້ອງນ້ຳ ຢູ່ ໃສ?
toilet is <u>where</u>

WHEN — MUHH'A DAII?   ເມື່ອໃດ

When are you going to Vang Viang?

<u>Muhh'a daii</u> jow si paii Wang Wiang?

ເມື່ອໃດ ເຈົ້າ ຊີ ໄປ ວັງວຽງ?

<u>when</u> you will go Vang Viang

WHY — PEN NYANG?   ເປັນ ຫຍັງ

Why do you think that?

<u>Pen nyang</u> jow kit naae'o nan?

ເປັນ ຫຍັງ ເຈົ້າ ຄິດ ແນວ ນັ້ນ?

You think that <u>why</u>

HOW — JANG DAII? / NAAEO DAII?   ຈັ່ງໃດ, ແນວໃດ

How do you say this in Lao?

An'nii paa'saa Laao wow <u>naae'o daii</u>?

ອັນ ນີ້ ພາສາ ລາວ ເວົ້າ <u>ແນວໃດ</u>?

thing this language Lao say <u>how</u>

HOW LONG — DON PAN DAII?   ດົນ ປານ ໃດ

How long is this bus ride?

<u>lik don pan daii</u> lot meh awwk?

ອີກ ດົນ ປານ ໃດ ລົດເມ ອອກ?

How long bus leave

HOW LONG ALREADY — DON LAAE'O?   ດົນ ແລ້ວ

Long time, no see.

<u>Don laae'o</u> tii (khawy) baw daii hen jow.

ດົນແລ້ວ ທີ່ (ຂ້ອຍ) ບໍ່ ໄດ້ ເຫັນ ເຈົ້າ

How long place no can see you

How long have you been in Laos?

Jow yuu (muhh'ang) Laao <u>don laae'o</u> baww?

ເຈົ້າຢູ່ (ເມືອງ) ລາວ <u>ດົນ ແລ້ວ</u> ບໍ່

You in (country) Laos How long

HOW MANY — JAK?/TOW DAII? ຈັກ/ເທົ່າ ໄດ

How old are you?

Jow aa'nyu jak pii?

ເຈົ້າ ອາຍຸ ຈັກ ປີ?

You age how many years

LIKE — MAAK + object ມັກ

I like it a lot.

Khawy mak laai.

ຂ້ອຍ ມັກ ຫຼາຍ

I like very

WANT

1) YAAK + verb ຍາກ + verb

Do you want to drink Beer Lao?

Jow yaak duhhm biaa Laao baww?

ເຈົ້າ ຍາກ ຕື່ມ ເບຍ ລາວ ບໍ່?

You want drink Beer Laao

2) YAAK + DAII + noun ຍາກ ໄດ້ + noun

I want money.

Khawy yaak daii ng´n.

ຂ້ອຍ ຍາກ ໄດ້ ເງິນ

I want money

3) YAAK + HAII + service you want ot expect of someone

Do you want me to help you with something?

Jow yaak haii khawy su'ai nyang baww ?

ເຈົ້າ ຍາກ ໃຫ້ ຂ້ອຍ ຊ່ວຍ ຫຍັງ ບໍ່?

You want give me help what

I'D LIKE / I'LL TAKE — OW + noun ເອົາ + noun

I'd like one Beer Lao.

<u>Ow</u> Biaa Laao gaae'o nuhng.

ເອົາ ເບຍ ລາວ ແກວ ໜຶ່ງ

<u>Take</u> Beer Lao bottle one

NEED + verb — DTAWNG GAN + verb ຕ້ອງການ + verb

I need to go.

Khawy <u>dtawng gan</u> paii.

ຂ້ອຍ <u>ຕ້ອງການ</u> ໄປ

I <u>want</u> go

SHOULD — KUAN JA ຄວນ ຈະ + verb

You should get a haircut.

Jow <u>kuan ja</u> paii dtat phom.

ເຈົ້າ <u>ຄວນ ຈະ</u> ໄປ ຕັດ ຜົມ

You <u>should</u> go cut hair

SUPPOSED TO — KUAN DTAWNG ຄວນ ຕ້ອງ + verb

You're supposed to do this.

Jow <u>kuan dtawng</u> het an'nii.

ເຈົ້າ <u>ຄວນ ຕ້ອງ</u> ເຮັດ ອັນນີ້

You <u>should</u> do this

HAVE TO — JAM PEN DTAWNG ຈຳ ເປັນ ຕ້ອງ + verb

I have to use the toilet.

Khawy <u>jam pen dtawng</u> saii hawng naam.

ຂ້ອຍ <u>ຈຳ ເປັນ ຕ້ອງ</u> ໃຊ້ ຫ້ອງ ນ້ຳ

I <u>have to</u> use toilet

MUST BE — KONG JA YUU + location ຄົງ ຈະ ຢູ່

He must be there already.

Laao kong ja yuu nan laae'o.

ລາວ ຄົງ ຈະ ຢູ່ ນັ້ນ ແລ້ວ

he must at there already

MUST BE — KONG JA PEN + adjectives or noun ຄົງ ຈະ ເປັນ

He <u>must be</u> tired.

Laao <u>kong ja pen</u> nuhh'ai

ລາວ ຄົງ ຈະ ເປັນ ເມື້ຍ

he <u>must be</u> tired

MAY — KHAWW ຂໍ

<u>May</u> I sit (here)?

Khawy <u>khaww</u> nang daii baww?

ຂ້ອຍ ຂໍ ນັ່ງ ໄດ້ ບໍ?

I may sit can

HOPE THAT — WANG WAA ຫວັງ ວ່າ

I <u>hope</u> you'll come again.

Khawy <u>wang waa</u> jow ja maa iik.

ຂ້ອຍ ຫວັງ ວ່າ ເຈົ້າ ຈະ ມາ ອີກ

I <u>hope</u> you will come again

THINK — KHIT ຄິດ

What do you <u>think</u>?

Jow <u>kit</u> nyang?

ເຈົ້າ ຄິດ ຫຍັງ?

You <u>think</u> what

THINK THAT — KHIT WAA ຄິດ ວ່າ

I think it is very pretty.

<u>Kit waa</u> ngaam laai.

ຄິດ ວ່າ ງາມ ຫຼ້າຍ

You <u>think</u> what

SPEAK — WOW ເວົ້າ

Please speak more slowly.

<u>Wow</u> saa'saa daae.

ເວົ້າ ຊ້າໆ ແທ່

<u>speak</u> slow slow

NOTE: **verbs** do not change according to tense.

   I go = I went = I am going

   Instead, other words are added:

I'm <u>going</u> to eat. ຈະ / ຊິ

   Khawy <u>ja/si</u> paii gin khow.

   ຂ້ອຍ ຈະ/ຊິ ໄປ ກິນ ເຂົ້າ.

   I will go eat food

I've <u>already</u> eaten. ແລ້ວ

   Khawy gin <u>laae'o.</u>

   ຂ້ອຍ ກິນ ແລ້ວ

   I eat already

Comparisions

LIKE — verb + KUHH   verb + ຄື

   You look <u>like</u> a movie star.

     Jow b´ng <u>kuhh</u> da'laa' nang.

     ເຈົ້າ ເບິ່ງ ຄື ດາລາໜັງ

     You look like movie star

ALSO/ SAME AS / TOO — KUHH'GAN ຄືກັນ

   You, <u>too.</u> (You also look like a movie star)

     Jow <u>kuhh'gan.</u>

     ເຈົ້າ <u>ຄືກັນ</u>

     You too

GUAA ກວ່າ (similar to the suffix -ER in English)

   She's smart<u>ER</u> than me.

     Laao sa'laat <u>gu'aa</u> khawy.

     ລາວ ສະຫຼາດ <u>ກວ່າ</u> ຂ້ອຍ

     she smart er than me

TII SUT ທີ ສຸດ (similar to the suffix **-EST** in English)

You're the <u>best</u> cook in the world.

    Jow pen kon kuaa gin tii geng <u>tii sut</u> naii look

    ເຈົ້າ ເປັນ ຄົນ ຄົວ ກິນ ທີ ເກັ່ງ ທີ ສຸດ ໃນ ໂລກ

Possessive

KHAWNG — ຂອງ

whose	khawg phaii?	ຂອງ ໃຜ
mine	khawng khawy	ຂອງ ຂ້ອຍ
yours	khawng jow	ຂອງ ເຈົ້າ
his/hers	khawng laao	ຂອງ ລາວ
theirs	khawng puak khow	ຂອງ ພວກເຂົາ
ours	khawng puak how	ຂອງ ເຮົາ

Sentence Endings

VERY — LAAI ຫຼາຍ

- Comes after an adjective.

I'm tired.	Khawy muhh'ai.	ຂ້ອຍ ເມື່ອຍ
I'm very tired.	Khawy muhh'ai laai	ຂ້ອຍ ເມື່ອຍ ຫຼາຍ

ALREADY—LAAE'O ແລ້ວ

- Comes after a verb or adjective.

I eat.	Khawy gin	ຂ້ອຍ ກິນ
I ate already.	Khawy gin laae'o.	ຂ້ອຍ ກິນ ແລ້ວ

- The contracted form of LAAE'O is LAE.

    Are you married <u>already</u>?

        Jow dtaaeng ngaan <u>laae'o</u> baww?

        ເຈົ້າ ແຕ່ງງານ ແລ້ວ ບໍ່?

        you married already

RIGHT?—HUH? NA ເນາະ

- Can be added to the end of any sentence.

    It's really hot, huh?!

    Hawn laai naw!?

    ຮ້ອນ ຫຼາຍ ເນາະ

    hot very huh

THANKS—DAAE, DERR ແດ່, ເດີ

- Often added to the end of a request or verbal appreciation.

    Can I speak with Nawy, please?

    Khaw wow gap Nawy daae?

    ຂໍ ເວົ້າ ກັບ ນ້ອຍ ແດ່

    may speak with Nawy please

Classifiers

- follow the quantity of the noun.

    I have three cats.

    Khawy mii maae'o saam <u>dtoo</u>.

    ຂ້ອຍ ມີ ແມວ ສາມ <u>ໂຕ</u>

    I have cat three <u>animals</u>

- The number one usually follows the classifier.

    I'll have a bottle of Beer Lao.

    Ow biaa Laao <u>gaae'o</u> nuhng.

    ເອົາ ເບຍ ລາວ <u>ແກ້ວ</u> ໜຶ່ງ

    take Beer Lao <u>bottle</u> one

animals, dogs, birds, aliens	dtoo	ໂຕ
boats & planes	lam	ລຳ
books, magazines	hu'aa	ຫົວ
bottles	gaae'o	ແກ້ວ
clothes, shirts, underwear	phuhhn	ຜືນ
buildings, houses, stores	lang	ຫຼັງ
electronics, fruit, furniture, cups	nu'ai	ໜ່ວຍ
flat items, paper, money	baii	ໃບ
long & thin wire, string	sen	ເສັ້ນ
knives & stamps	du'ang	ດວງ
pairs, jeans, shoes	kuu	ຄູ່
people	kon	ຄົນ
silverware, fork & spoon	gaan	ກ້ານ
things	an	ອັນ
vehicles, cars, bikes	kan	ຄັນ

XXIV. Tones & Alphabet

Consonants

Alphabetical order of consonants as found in Dictionary:

1.	ກ	18.	ຜ
2.	ຂ	19.	ຝ
3.	ຄ	20.	ພ
4.	ງ	21.	ຟ
5.	ຈ	22.	ມ
6.	ສ	23.	ຢ
7.	ຊ	24.	ຣ
8.	ດ	25.	ຫງ
9.	ຕ	26.	ຫຍ
10.	ຖ	27.	ຫນ
11.	ທ	28.	ຫມ
12.	ນ	29.	ໜ / ຫລ
13.	ບ	30.	ຫວ
14.	ປ	31.	ອ
15.	ຜ	32.	ຮ
16.	ຝ		
17.	ພ		

Note: The letter r (R), at one time removed from the alphabet, is making a comeback.

Vowels

Vowels in alphabetical order as found in dictionary:

1. Xะ		21. XɔX
2. X̌X		22. G X̃
3. Xๅ		23. G X̃
4. X̃		24. G X̌ʂะ
5. X̃		25. X̌ʂX
6. X̃		26. GXʊ, (G X̌ʂ)
7. X̃		27. Xʂ X
8. X̦		28. G X̃ə
9. X̦		29. G X̃ə
10. GXะ		30. X̌ɔะ
11. GX̌X		31. X̌ɔะ
12. GX		32. X̌ɔ
13. GGXะ		33. XɔX
14. GGX̌X		34. ʔX
15. GGX		35. ʟX
16. ʟXะ		36. G X̃ๅ
17. X̃X		37. X́ๅ
18. ʟX		38. XəʊU
19. GXๅะ		
20. Ẋ		

Tones

Consonants in tonal groups:

Low Tones	High Tones	Rising Tones
ກ	ຄ	ຂ
ຈ	ງ	ສ
ດ	ຊ	ຖ
ຕ	ຍ	ຜ
ບ	ທ	ຝ
ປ	ນ	ຫ
ຢ	ພ	Special Spellings with rising tones
ອ	ຟ	
	ມ	ຫງ
	ລ	ຫຍ
	ວ	ໜ
	ຮ	ໝ
		ຫຼ or ຫລ

- Words beginning with low consonants have a *low* sound.
- Words beginning with high Consonants have a *high* sound.
- Words beginning with rising cconsonants *rise.*

There are *four* tonal marks that may be placed over Lao words, but only two are regularly used.

The first tonal symbol is called MAI TOO ໄມ້ໂທ. It looks like a squiggly number 2 with a long tail (້). When this is placed over a letter it causes the sound to fall.

The second tonal symbol is called MAI EIK, ໄມ້ເອກ. It looks like a short number 1 placed over a letter (່). It causes a middle high tone.

The third is mai jatdtawaa ໄມ້ຈັດຕະວາ (.) and the fourth is Mai dtii ໄມ້ຕີ (๏). The former looks like a lower-case "m" with a tail and the latter looks like "a "+ sign. They are both rarely used and change the sound to a short "pop!"

Tones + Close sound

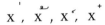

x , x , x , x

Be careful of the following:

far, chicken, near
ໄກ, ໄກ່, ໃກ້
gaii, gaii, gaii

I, water buffalo, penis
ຂ້ອຍ, ຄວາຍ, ໂຄຍ
khawy, ku'aai, koy

love, vomit
ຮັກ, ຮາກ
hak, haak

Excuse me, I broke wind
ຂໍໂທດ, ຂ້ອຍຕົດ
Khaww Toot, Khawy dtot

fish, forest, aunt
ປາ, ປ່າ, ປ້າ
baa, baa, baa

silk, new
ໄໝ, ໃໝ່
maii, mai

Notes

ก

at the beginning sounds like **G**

at the end sounds like **K** (but nearly silent)

บ

at the beginning sounds like **B**

at the end sounds like P (but nearly silent)

ด

at the beginning sounds like **D**

at the end sounds like **T** (but nearly silent)

อ

at the beginning sounds like **W**

at the end sounds like **O** as in a soft oh

ย

at beginning sounds like **NY** as in onion

at end sounds like **E** as in be, he, see (but is quite short)

ฮ

This is a neutral consonant / vowel. Between two letters, it takes the sound of **AW**. It becomes silent when accompanied with a vowel and only the vowel is voiced.

The 3 sounds below stay the same at the beginning and end of any word:

ม	m
น	n
ง	ng

xxv. Cards

Cards games are a common from of entertainment in Laos and often include gambling small amount of cash. Also, in games of fortune, the black suite are always "undesireable" as opposed to due red one.

Card	paii	ໄພ່
Ace	maak aaet	ໝາກແອັດ
2	maak sawng	ໝາກສອງ
3	maak saam	ໝາກສາມ
4	maak sii	ໝາກສີ່
5	maak haa	ໝາກຫ້າ
6	maak hok	ໝາກຫົກ
7	maak jet	ໝາກເຈັດ
8	maak paaet	ໝາກແປດ
9	maak gow	ໝາກເກົ້າ
10	maak sip	ໝາກສິບ
J	maak boy	ໝາກໂບ່ຍ
Q	maak dam	ໝາກດຳ
K	maak thow	ໝາກເຖົ້າ

Spade	bit	ບິດ
Club	juan	ຈ່ວມ
Heart	gerr	ເກີ
Diamond	loo	ໂລ

Do you want to play cards?

Jow yaak lin paii baww?

ເຈົ້າຢາກຫຼິ້ນໄພ້ບໍ່?

shuffle	saak	ສາກ
cut	dtat	ຕັດ
deal	yaa'i	ຢາຍ
draw	ju'aa	ຈ່ອ
your turn.	tii Jow	ທີ່ເຈົ້າ
go again.	paii iik	ໄປອີກ
point(s)	ka naaen	ຄະແນນ
throw	thim	ຖິ້ມ
lower	dtaam gu'aa	ຕ່ຳກວ່າ
higher	nyai gu'aa	ໃຫຍ່ກວ່າ
same	kuhh gan	ຄືກັນ
special	pi sayt	ພິເສດ
win	sa'na	ຊະນະ
lose	siaa, paae	ເສຍ, ແພ້

XXVII. Dictionary

Kam sap ຄຳສັບ

A

above	taang tuhng	ທາງເທິງ
accent	awwk siang	ອອກຊຽງ
accident	u'bat dti hayt	ອຸບັດຕິເຫດ
accuse (v)	gaao toot	ກາວໂທດ
across	khaam	ຂ້າມ
addict	phuu sayp dtit	ຜູ້ເຂບຕິດ
address (n)	tii yuu	ທີ່ຢູ່
adjust	pap bung	ປັບປຸງ
admit (confess)	nyawm hap	ຍອມຮັບ
adult	phuu nyaii	ຜູ້ໃຫຍ່
advantage	gaan daii	ການໄດ້
afraid	yaan	ย้าม
after	lang jaak	ຫລັງຈາກ
again	iik tuhh'a nuhng	ອີກເທື່ອນື່ງ
air	aa'gaat	ອາກາດ
airport	sa'naam biin	ສະໜາມບິນ
alcohol	lao	ເຫລົ້າ
all	tang mot	ທັງໝົດ
alphabet	pa nya'n sa'na	ພະຍັນຊະນະ
already	laae'o	ແລ້ວ
always	sa merr	ສະເໝີ
amnesia	kuaam jaam suhh'am	ຄວາມຈຳເສື່ອມ
amount	luam	ລວມ
ancestor	ban pa buu lut	ບັນພະບູລຸດ
and	laae	ແລະ

angry	jaii haai	ໃຈຮ້າຍ
another	iik	ອີກ
answer (v)	dtawp	ຕອບ
ant	mot	ມົດ
anthem	payng saat	ເພງຊາດ
antique	boo laan (wat thu)	ໂບລານ (ວັດຖຸ)
anxious	hawn jaii	ຮ້ອນໃຈ
anybody	phuu daii phhuu nuhng	ຜູ້ໃດຜູ້ໜຶ່ງ
anything	sing nuhhng	ສິ່ງໜຶ່ງ
anywhere	tii daii daii	ທີ່ໃດໆ
apple	maak aep'buhhn	ໝາກແອບເປິ້ນ
approximately	pa maan	ປະມານ
area	puhhn tii	ພື້ນທີ່
argue	dtoo thiang	ໂຕ້ຖຽງ
arm	khaaen	ແຂນ
arrive	maa hawt	ມາຮອດ
at	tii	ທີ່
aunt	baa, aa, naa saao	ປ້າ, ອາ, ນ້າສາວ
average	kit sa liaa	ຄິດສະເລ່ຍ
awful	pen dtaa waat li'ow	ເປັນຕາຫວາດສຽວ

B

baby	dek nawy nawy	ເດັກນ້ອຍໆ
bad (not good)	baww dii	ບໍ່ດີ
bag (plastic)	thong	ຖົງ
bag (travel)	ga'bow	ກະເປົ໋າ
ball	maak baan	ໝາກບານ
bamboo	maii phaii	ໄມ້ໄຜ່
banana	maak gu'ai	ໝາກກ້ວຍ
bandage	phaa pan phaae	ຜ້າພັນແຜ
bank	ta'naa'kaan	ທະນາຄານ
bar	baa duhhm laao	ບາດື່ມເຫຼົ້າ
barber	saang dtat phom	ຊ່າງຕັດຜົມ
basket	ga dtaa	ກະຕາ

basketball	gi'laa baats'guhht	ກິລາບາດສເກັດ
bat (bird)	(doo) jiaa	(ໂດ) ຈະຍ
battery	maam fhaii/ thaan	ໝ້ຳໄຟ/ຖານ
beautiful	ngaam	ງາມ
because	paw waa	ເພາະວ່າ
bed	dtiang nawn	ຕຽງນອນ
beef	siin ngu'aa	ຊີ້ນງົວ
beer	biaa	ເບຍ
before	gawn	ກ່ອນ
beggar	kon khaww taan	ຄົນຂໍທານ
believe	suhh'a (tuhh)	ເຊື່ອ (ຖື)
belt	saai aae'o	ຂາຍແອວ
best	dii tii sut	ດີທີ່ສຸດ
bet	pa nan	ພະນັນ
better	dii gua'a	ດີກ່ວາ
big	nyaii	ໃຫຍ່
bike	lot thiip	ລົດຖີບ
bill (check)	baii hap ng´n/ baii bin	ໃບຮັບເງິນ/ໃບບິນ
bird	nok	ນົກ
bite	gat	ກັດ
black	muhht/sii daam	ມຶດ/ສີດຳ
blanket	phaa hom	ຜ້າຫົ່ມ
bleach	naw yaa sak phaa khow	ນ້ຳຢາຊັກຜ້າຂາວ
blind	dtaa bawt	ຕາບອດ
blood	luhh'at	ເລືອດ
blowdry	daii (phom)	ໄດ (ຜົມ)
blue	sii fhaa	ສີຟ້າ
boat	huhh'a	ເຮືອ
body (p. 92)	haang gaai	ຮ່າງກາຍ
bomb	la buhht	ລະເບີດ
book	puhhm	ປື້ມ
border	saai daaen	ຂາຍແດນ
boring	buhh'a	ເບື່ອ
borrow	yuhhm	ຍືມ

boss	hu'aa naa	ຫົວໜ້າ
both	taang sawg	ທັງສອງ
bother	(lop) gu'an	(ລົບ) ກວນ
bottom	puhhn lum	ພື້ນລຸມ
box	gap/ hiip	ກັບ/ຫີບ
boy	dek nawy phuu saai	ເດັກນ້ອຍຜູ້ຊາຍ
brain	sa mawng	ສະໝອງ
bread	khow jii	ເຂົ້າຈີ
break	dtaaek/ hak	ແຕກ/ຫັກ
bring	ow maa	ເອົາມາ
brother	aai/ nawng saai	ອ້າຍ/ນ້ອງຊາຍ
buddha	pa put ta jow	ພະພຸດທະເຈົ້າ
buddhism	put'ta saa'sa'naa	ພຸດທະສາສະໝາ
bug	maaeng maii	ແມງໄມ້
bullet	luuk puhhn	ລູກປືນ
business	tu'la'git	ທຸລະກິດ
but	dtaae waa	ແຕ່ວ່າ
buy	suhh	ຊື້

C

call (name)	hawng/ errn	ຮ້ອງ/ເອີ້ນ
call (phone)	too haa	ໂທຣສັບ
camera	gawng thaai huup	ກ້ອງຖ່າຍຮູບ
can (able)	daii	ໄດ້
candle	tian khaii	ທຽນໄຂ
car	lot nyaii	ລົດໃຫຍ່
cards	paii	ໄພ່
careful!	La wang	ລະວັງ
cat	maae'o	ແມວ
catholic	saa'sa'naa kaaet'too'lik	ສາສະໝາແຄດໂທລິກ
cemetary	paa saa	ປ່າຊ້າ
centimeter	sang dtii maaet	ຊັງຕີແມັດ
center	jaii gaang	ໃຈກາງ
chair	dtang	ຕັ່ງ

change (v)	pian	ປ່ຽນ
cheap	(laa kaa) thuhhk	(ລາຄາ) ຖືກ
chicken	gaii	ໄກ່
child	dek nawy	ເດັກນ້ອຍ
chillies	makk phet	ໝາກເຜັດ
choose	luhh'ak	ເລືອກ
chopsticks	maii thuu	ໄມ້ຖູ່
christian	saa'sa'naa'kliit	ສາສະໜາຄຼິດ
cigarette	yaa suup	ຢາສູບ
city	muhh'ang	ເມືອງ
clean (v)	het haii sa'aat	ເຮັດໃຫ້ລະອາດ
climb	piin/dtaii	ປີນ/ໄຕ່
close (v)	bit/jop	ປິດ/ຈົບ
close (adj)	gaii (sit)	ໃກ້ (ຊິດ)
clothes	kuhh'ang nung	ເຄື່ອງນຸ່ງ
coat	suhh'a nyaii	ເສື້ອໃຫຍ່
cold	noww	ໜາວ
color	sii	ສີ
comb	wii (phom)	ຫວີ (ຜົມ)
come	maa	ມາ
comfortable	sa'duak sa'baai	ສະດວກສະບາຍ
company	baww'li'sat	ບໍລິສັດ
complain	dtaww'waa	ຕໍ່ວ່າ
computer	kuam'piu'dterr	ຄອມພິວເຕີ
conditioner	kiim nuat phom	ຄີມນວດຜົມ
confident	kuaam waii waang jaii	ຄວາມໄວ້ວາງໃຈ
confusing	sap son	ສັບສົນ
constipation	tawng phu	ທ້ອງຜູ
contradiction	wow baw khow gan	ເວົ້າບໍ່ເຂົ້າກັນ
cook (n) m/f	paww kuaa/maae kuaa	ພໍຄົວ/ແມ່ຄົວ
cook (v)	kuaa gin	ຄົວກິນ
cotton	fhaai	ຝ້າຍ
cough	aii	ໄອ
country (p. 19)	pa'tayt	ປະເທດ
countryside	baan´nawwk	ບ້ານນອກ

cow	ngu'aa	ງົວ
crazy	phii baa	ຜີບ້າ
cup	jawk	ຈອກ
custom	pa pay nii	ປະເພນີ
cut	dtat	ຕັດ

D

dangerous	an'dta'laai	ອັນຕະລາຍ
dare	gaa haan/taa taai	ກ້າຫານ/ທ້າທາຍ
dark	muhht/kaam	ມືດ/ຄໍ່າ
date	wan tii	ວັນທີ
daughter	luuk saao	ລູກສາວ
day	muhh	ມື້
dead	dtaai laae'o	ຕາຍແລ້ວ
deaf	huu nu'ak	ຫູໜວກ
decide	dtat sin jaii	ຕັດສິນໃຈ
deep	l'k	ເລິກ
delicious	saaep	ແຊບ
democracy	pa'saa'ti'bpa'dtaii	ປະຊາທິປະໄຕ
dentist	maww pu'aa khaae'o	ໝໍປົວແຂ້ວ
depressed	siaa jaii	ເສຍໃຈ
detergent	fhaaep	ແຟບ
dialect	saam niang	ສຳນຽງ
diarrhea	thawk tawng	ຖອກທ້ອງ
dice	maak dtao	ໝາກເຕົ໋າ
die	dtaai	ຕາຍ
different	dtaaek dtaang	ແຕກຕ່າງ
difficult	nyaak	ຍາກ
dirty	puhh'an	ເປື້ອນ
discount	lut	ຫຼຸດ
disk	diis gaaet	ດິສແກ໋ດ
dive	dam naam	ດຳນ້ຳ
divorce	pa hang	ປະຮ້າງ
dizzy	win huaa/muhn	ວິນຫົວ/ມຶນ

do	het	ເຮັດ
doctor	taan maww	ທ່ານໝໍ
dog	maa	ໝາ
don't	baw het	ບໍ່ເຮັດ
door	pa'dtuu	ປະຕູ
down	long (maa)	ລົງ (ມາ)
draw	dtaaem	ແຕ້ມ
dream	fhan	ຝັນ
dress	ga'poong	ກະໂປ່ງ
drive	khap	ຂັບ
dry	(haaeng) laaeng	(ແຫ້ງ) ແລ້ງ

E

earth	look/phaaen din	ໂລກ/ແຜ່ນດິນ
east	tit dtaa wen awwk	ທິດຕາເວັນອອກ
eat	gin	ກິນ
economy	gaan pa yat	ການປະຍັດ
egg	khaii	ໄຂ່
elect	luhh'ak (dtang)	ເລືອກ (ຕັ້ງ)
electricity	fhaii fhaa	ໄຟຟ້າ
embarrass	uht at jaii	ອຶດອັດໃຈ
embassy	sa'thaan tuut	ສະຖານທູດ
empty	waang pow	ຫວ່າງເປົ່າ
engine	kuhh'ang jak	ເຄື່ອງຈັກ
English	ang'git	ອັງກິດ
enjoy	mu'an suhhn/puhht puhhn	ມວນຊື່ນ/ເພີດເພີນ
enough	piang paww/paww laaeo	ພຽງພໍ/ພໍແລ້ວ
enter	khow paii	ເຂົ້າໄປ
entertainment	khu'aam puhht puhhn	ຄວາມເພີດເພີນ
envelope(s)	sawng jot maai	ຊອງຈົດໝາຍ
envy	it saa	ອິດສາ
equal	tao gap	ເທົ່າກັບ
escape	liik nii/liik liang	ຫຼີກໜີ/ຫຼີກລຽງ
etiquette	maa la nyaat	ມາລະຍາດ
evening	dtawn laaeng	ຕອນແລງ

every	tuk tuk	ທຸກໆ
exactly	taae jing/naae nawn	ແທ້ຈິງ/ແນ່ນອນ
exam	gaan sawp seng	ການສອບເສັ້ງ
exchange	gaan laaek pian	ການແລກປ່ຽນ
exchange rate	at'dtaa laaek pian	ອັດຕາແລກປ່ຽນ
excuse me	khaww toot	ຂໍໂທດ
exit	taang awwk	ທາງອອກ
expensive	(laa kaa) paaeng	(ລາຄາ) ແພງ
explorer	sam luat/kon haa	ສຳຫລວດ/ຄົນຫາ
explosion	la buhht dtaaek	ລະເບີດແຕກ
eye	dtaa	ຕາ

F

fabric	phaa	ຜ້າ
face	naa	ຫນ້າ
fake	khawng pawm	ຂອງປອມ
fall	dtok	ຕົກ
family	kawp kua'a	ຄອບຂົວ
fan	pat (lom)	ພັດ (ລົມ)
far	gaii	ໄກ
fast	waii	ໄວ
fat	dtui/mii khaii man	ຕຸ້ຍ/ມີໄຂມັນ
father	paww	ພໍ່
fax	fhaaek	ແຟກ
feed (animals)	liang	ລ້ຽງ
feel	(kuaam) huu suhk	(ຄວາມ) ຮູ້ສຶກ
ferry	huhh'a hap jaang	ເຮືອຮັບຈ້າງ
festival	ngaan sa'lawng	ງານສະຫຼອງ
fever	khaii	ໄຂ້
field	tong naa	ທົ່ງນາ
find (v)	sawk haa	ຊອກຫາ
fire (n)	fhaii	ໄຟ
fire from job	laii awwk	ໄລ່ອອກ
fish	paa	ປາ
fix	sawm paaeng	ສ້ອມແປງ

flag	tunng	ທຸງ
flat	li'ap/paae	ລຽບ/ແປ
flat tire	yaang lot huu'a	ຍາງລົດຮ່ວ
floor	puhhn/san	ພື້ນ/ຊັ້ນ
flour	paaeng	ແປ້ງ
flower	dawk maii	ດອກໄມ້
flush	got sak kook	ກົດຊັກໂຄກ
fly (v)	bin	ບິນ
fly/ insect (n)	maaeng wan	ແມງວັນ
food	aa'haan	ອາຫານ
foot	dtiin	ຕີນ
foreigner	fha'lang	ຝະລັ່ງ
forever	dta'lawt pai	ຕະລອດໄປ
forget	luhhm	ລືມ
fork	sawm	ສ້ອມ
fountain	naam puu	ນ້ຳພຸ
free	waang	ຫວ່າງ
free of charge	fhii	ຟີ
friend	muu	ຫມູ່
Friendship Bridge	khu'aa miit'dta'paap	ຂົວມິດຕະພາບ
from	maa jaak	ມາຈາກ
fruit (p. 62)	maak maii	ຫມາກໄມ້
full	dtem	ເຕັມ
fun	mu'an suhhn	ມ່ວນຊື່ນ
furniture	kuhh'ang dtaaeng baan	ເຄື່ອງແຕ່ງບ້ານ
future	aa'naa kot	ອານາຄົດ

G

gamble	pa'nan	ພະນັນ
game	gayym	ເກມ
garbage	khii nyuhh'a	ຂີ້ເຫຍື້ອ
gas	gaaes	ແກ໊ສ
gas (petrol)	naam ma'an	ນ້ຳມັນ
get	ow	ເອົາ

gift	khawng khu'an	ຂອງຂັນ
ginger	khiing	ຂີງ
girl/boyfriend	fhaaen	ແຟນ
give	ow haii	ເອົາໃຫ້
glass (cup)	jawk	ຈອກ
go	paii	ໄປ
god	pa'jow/tay'wa'daa	ພະເຈົ້າ/ເທວະດາ
gold	kaam	ຄຳ
good	dii	ດີ
grade level(n)	laam dap	ລຳດັບ
graduate (v)	daii hap pa'lin'nyaa	ໄດ້ຮັບປະລິນຍາ
great (large)	nyaii/saam kan	ໃຫຍ່/ສຳຄັນ
green	sii khi'ow	ສີຂຽວ
ground	khii din	ຂີ້ດິນ
grow	nyaii khuhhn/ngawk ngaam	ໃຫຍ່ຂຶ້ນ/ງອກງາມ
guarantee	gaan hap'pa gan	ການຮັບປະກັນ
guard (n)	kon nyaam	ຄົນຍາມ
guard (v)	fhow hak saa	ເຝົ້າຮັກສາ
guide (n)	phuu naam ti'ow	ຜູ້ນຳທ່ຽວ
guide (v)	haii naae'o taang	ໃຫ້ແນວທາງ
gum	sing om	ສິ່ງອົມ
gun	puhhn	ປືນ
gym	bawn awwk gaam lang gaai	ບ່ອນອອກກຳລັງກາຍ

H

hair (head,skin)	phom/khon	ຜົມ/ຂົນ
haircut	dtat phom	ຕັດຜົມ
hammok	payy/uu	ເປ/ອູ່
hand	muhh	ມື
handsome	jow suu/laww	ເຈົ້າຊູ້/ຫຼໍ່
hang	khu'aaen/hawy	ແຂວນ/ຫ້ອຍ
hanger	yu'ang gaw!	່ຢ່ວງເກາະ

happy	dii jaii/nyin dii	ດີໃຈ/ຍິນດີ
hard	khaaeng	ແຂງ
hat	mu'ak	ໝວກ
have	mii	ມີ
head	hu'aa	ຫົວ
hear	daii nyin	ໄດ້ຍິນ
heart	hu'aa jaii	ຫົວໃຈ
heat (adj)	ku'aam hawn	ຄວາມຮ້ອນ
heat up (v)	hawn khuhhn	ຮ້ອນຂຶ້ນ
heaven	sa'wan	ສະຫວັນ
hello	sa'baai dii	ສະບາຍດີ
helmet	mu'ak gan nawk	ໝວກກັນໜ່ອກ
help	suai luhh'a	ຊ່ວຍເຫຼືອ
her	laao (phuu nying)	ລາວ (ຜູ້ຍິງ)
hers	khawng laao (phuu nying)	ຂອງລາວ (ຜູ້ຍິງ)
here	yuu nii	ຢູ່ນີ້
hero	wi la buu lut/pa ayk	ວິລະບຸລຸດ/ພະເອກ
hide	lii/ bang/suhh'ang	ລີ້/ບັງ/ເຊື່ອງ
high	suung	ສູງ
hill	nuhhn puu	ເນີນພູ
him	laao (phuu saai)	ລາວ (ຜູ້ຊາຍ)
his	khawng laao (phuu saai)	ຂອງລາວ (ຜູ້ຊາຍ)
history	pa wat saat	ປະຫວັດສາດ
hit	dtii	ຕີ
hobby	ngaan a'dii layt	ງານອະດິເລກ
hold	thuhh/wi	ຖື/ຫິ້ວ
hole	huu	ຮູ
home	huhh'an	ເຮືອນ
honk	gaae lot	ແກເລັດ
hook(n)	khaww	ຂໍ
hope(v)	wang waa	ຫວັງວ່າ
hostel	baan pak	ບ້ານພັກ
hot	hawn	ຮ້ອນ
hotel	hoong haaen	ໂຮງແຮມ

hour(ly)	su'aa moong	ຊົ່ວໂມງ
house	huhh'an/baan	ເຮືອນ/ບ້ານ
how	naae'o daii / baaep daii	ແນວໃດ/ແບບໃດ
how much?	tao daii?	ເທົ່າໃດ
hungry	hiu khow	ຫິວເຂົ້າ
(it) hurts	jep	ເຈັບ

I

I	khawy	ຂ້ອຍ
ice	naam gawn	ນ້ຳກ້ອນ
idea	ku'aam kit	ຄວາມຄິດ
if	thaa (waa)	ຖ້າ (ວ່າ)
ill	jep nak	ເຈັບໜັກ
illegal	phit got maai	ຜິດກົດໝາຍ
immigration	gom gu'at kon khow muhh'ang	ກົມກວດຄົນເຂົ້າເມືອງ
immoral	phit sin la taam	ຜິດສິນລະທຳ
impatient	baw ot'ton	ບໍ່ອົດທົນ
imply	sa'daaeng thuh'waa	ສະແດງເຖິງວ່າ
impossible	pen paii baw daii	ເປັນໄປບໍ່ໄດ້
in	yuu naii	ຢູ່ໃນ
include	luam tang/nap taang	ລວມທັງ/ນັບທາງ
income(monthly)	ng´n duhh'an	ເງິນເດືອນ
inconsiderate	phuu baw kit thuhng jaii phuu uhhn	ຜູ້ບໍ່ຄິດເຖິງໃຈຜູ້ອື່ນ
inconvenient	baw sa'duak	ບໍ່ສະດວກ
incorrect	baw thuhhk	ບໍ່ຖືກ
independent	ayk'ga'laat	ເອກະລາດ
indifferent	baw ow jaii saii	ບໍ່ເອົາໃຈໃສ່
inferior	dtam gu'aa/dawy gu'aa	ຕ່ຳກວ່າ/ດ້ອຍກວ່າ
injury	baat jep	ບາດເຈັບ
innertube	gong yaang	ກົງຢາງ
innocent	laii diang saa	ໄລ່ດຽງສາ
inside	yuu naii	ຢູ່ໃນ

insurance	pa gan paii	ປະກັນໄພ
intelligent	sa'laat	ສະຫຼາດ
interesting	naa son jaii	ໜ້າສົນໃຈ
international	paai nawk/saa gon	ພາຍນອກ/ສາກົນ
Internet	in'dterr'net	ອິນເຕີເນັດ
interrupt	khat jang wa	ຂັດຈັງວະ
introduce	naae'naam	ແນະນຳ
invent	pa dit/kit khuhhn	ປະດິດ/ຄິດຂຶ້ນ
invisible	gaam bang	ກຳບັງ
iron (n)	dtao liit	ເຕົາລີດ
irrational	baw mii hayt phon	ບໍ່ມີເຫດຜົນ
island	gaw/dawn	ເກາະ/ດອນ
it	man	ມັນ
itch (v)	ka	ຄາ

J

jacket	suhh'a nawk	ເສື້ອນອກ
jade	yok	ຢົກ
jail	kuk/bawn gak khang	ຄຸກ/ບ່ອນກັກຂັງ
jealous	it'saa / huhng	ອິດສາ/ຫຶງ
jewelry	khuhh'ang pa dap	ເຄື່ອງປະດັບ
Jewish	saa'sa'naa yiu	ສາສະໜາຢິວ
job, work (p 27)	wiak	ວຽກ
juice	naam maak maii	ນ້ຳໝາກໄມ້

K

keep	hak saa	ຮັກສາ
key	ga'jaae	ກະແຈ
kick	dte	ເຕະ
kill	khaa	ຂ້າ
king	jow sii'wit	ເຈົ້າຊີວິດ
knife	miit	ມີດ
know	huu (jak)	ຮູ້ (ຈັກ)

130

L

language	paa'saa	ພາສາ
last	sut'taai	ສຸດທ້າຍ
last night	muhh'kuhh'n nii	ມື້ຄືນນີ້
late	saa/maa saa	ຊ້າ/ມາຊ້າ
laugh	hu'aa khu'an	ຫົວຂ້ວນ
law	got maai	ກົດໝາຍ
laxative	yaa thaai/ yaa la'baai	ຢາຖ່າຍ/ຢາລະບາຍ
lazy	khii'kaan	ຂີ້ຄ້ານ
learn	hian (huu)	ຮຽນ (ຮູ້)
leave	jaak paii	ຈາກໄປ
left side	buhh'ang saai	ເບື້ອງຊ້າຍ
lend	haii yuhhm	ໃຫ້ຢືມ
letter	jot maai	ຈົດໝາຍ
license	baii a'nu nyaat	ໃບອະນຸຍາດ
license plate	paai lot	ປ້າຍລົດ
lick	liaa	ເລຍ
lie (v)	(khii) dtua	(ຂີ້) ຕົວະ
life	sii'wit	ຊີວິດ
light	saaeng sa'waang	ແສງສະຫວ່າງ
like (v)	mak	ມັກ
listen	fhang	ຟັງ
little	nawy	ນ້ອຍ
(A) little	nawy nuhng	ໜ້ອຍໜຶ່ງ
live	yuu/pak	ຢູ່/ພັກ
local	tawng thuhhn	ທ້ອງຖິ່ນ
lock (n)	khang	ຂັງ
lock (v)	lawk ga'jaae	ລ໊ອກກະແຈ
long	nyow	ຍາວ
look	buhng	ເບິ່ງ
look for	sawk haa	ຊອກຫາ
lose	siaa	ເສຍ
lost (adj)	long taang	ຫຼົງທາງ
loud	siang dang/fhot	ສຽງດັງ/ຟົດ

love	hak	ຮັກ
low	dtam	ຕ່ຳ
lucky	sook dii	ໂຊກດີ

M

mad (angry)	jaii haai	ໃຈຮ້າຍ
magic	maa yaa gon/	ມາຍາກົນ/
	way mon/kaa thaa	ເວດມົນ/ຄາຖາ
mail(v)	song paii'sa'nii	ສົ່ງໄປສະນີ
make	het/ga'taam	ເຮັດ/ກະທຳ
man	phuu saai	ຜູ້ຊາຍ
Manners	maa la nyaat	ມາລະຍາດ
many	laai	ຫຼາຍ
map	paaen tii	ແຜນທີ່
market	dta'laat	ຕະຫຼາດ
marriage	dtaaeng'ngaan	ແຕ່ງງານ
martyr	phuu siaa sa la	ຜູ້ເສຍສະຫຼະ
marxism	tit sa dii khawng maak	ທິດສະດີຂອງມາກ
match(for fire)	maii khiit fhaii/	ໄມ້ຂີດໄຟ
match (sport)	gaan khaaeng khan	ການແຂ່ງຂັນ
maybe	baang tii	ບາງທີ
me	khawy	ຂ້ອຍ
measure	khuhh'ang wat taaek	ເຄື່ອງວັດແທກ
meet	pop/jer	ພົບ/ເຈີ
mekong	maae naam khawng	ແມ່ນ້ຳຂອງ
menu	laai gaan aa'haan	ລາຍການອາຫານ
milk	nom	ນົມ
mine	khawng khawy	ຂອງຂ້ອຍ
minute	naa'tii	ນາທີ
mirror	waaen nyaaeng	ແວ່ນແຍງ
mistake	phit	ຜິດ
mobile phone	muhh tuh	ມືທື
money	ng´n	ເງິນ
month	duhh'an	ເດືອນ

monument	aa'nu saa'wa'lii	ອານຸສາວະລີ
moon	(duang) duhh'an	(ດວງ) ເດືອນ
morals	sin taam	ສິນທຳ
more	puhhm/iik	ເພີ້ມ/ອີກ
morning (market)	(dta'laat) sao	(ຕະຫຼາດ) ເຊົ້າ
mother	maae	ແມ່
motor	khuhh'ang jak	ເຄື່ອງຈັກ
motorbike	lot jak	ລົດຈັກ
mountain	puu	ພູ
move	nyaai	ຍ້າຍ
Mr.	taan/taao	ທ່ານ/ທ້າວ
Mrs.	(taan) naang	(ທ່ານ) ນາງ
museum	haww pi pit dta paan	ຫໍພິພິດຕະພານ
music	don dtii	ດົນຕີ

N

name	suhh	ຊື່
napkin (paper)	tiis'suu	ທິສຊູ
nation	saat	ຊາດ
nationalism	saat ni nyom/	ຊາດນິຍົມ/
	ku'aam pen saat	ຄວາມເປັນຊາດ
nausea	aa'gaan pun tawng	ອາການປັ່ນທ້ອງ
near	gaii	ໃກ້
need (v)	jaam pen	ຈຳເປັນ
needle	khem	ເຂັມ
nervous	khu'an awwn	ຂວັນອ່ອນ
net	dtaa naang	ຕາໜ່າງ
never	baw khuhh'y	ບໍ່ເຄີຍ
nevermind	baw pen' nyang	ບໍ່ເປັນຫຍັງ
new	maii	ໃໝ່
no	baww	ບໍ່
nobody	baw mii phaii	ບໍ່ມີໃຜ
North	tit nuhh'a	ທິດເໜືອ
not yet	nyaang	ຍັງ

nothing	baw mii nyaang	ບໍ່ມີຫຍາງ
now	diao nii	ດຽວນີ້
number (p.97)	dtu'aa layk	ຕົວເລກ

O

obnoxious	naa lang giat	ໜ້າລັງກຽດ
of course	naae nawn	ແນ່ນອນ
oil	naam man	ນ້ຳມັນ
old	thow/gaae/sa'laa	ເຖົ້າ/ແກ່/ສະລາ
on	yuu tuhng	ຢູ່ເທິງ
once	kang nuhhng	ຄັ້ງໜຶ່ງ
only	piang dtaae	ພຽງແຕ່
only one	an di'ow	ອັນດຽວ
open	buhht	ເປີດ
opinion	ku'am khit hen	ຄວາມຄິດເຫັນ
opportunity	oo'gaat	ໂອກາດ
or	luhh (waa)	ຫຼື (ວ່າ)
ordinary	taam ma daa	ທຳມະດາ
original	khawng taae	ຂອງແທ້
other	uhhn uhhn	ອື່ນໆ
outside	khaang nawk	ຂ້າງນອກ
owe	pen nii	ເປັນໜີ້

P

pack (v)	haww	ຫໍ່
paper	jiaa	ເຈ້ຍ
paranoid	pen gang wan	ເປັນກາງວັນ
park(n)	sawn saa tha la	ສວນສາທາລະ
park a car (v)	bawn jawt lot	ບ່ອນຈອດລົດ
party (festive)	ngaan liang	ງານລ້ຽງ
party (government)	pak gaan muhh'ang	ພັກການເມື່ອງ
patient (n)	kon pu'ai/kon khaii	ຄົນປວຍ/ຄົນໄຂ້
patient (adj)	khua'am ot'ton	ຄວາມອົດທົນ
pay (v)	jaai	ຈ່າຍ

peace	sin su'an/san tii paap	ຂີ້ສວນ/ສັນທິພາບ
pen	bik	ບິກ
perfect	som buun	ສົມບຸນ
person	kon	ຄົນ
pharmacy	haan khaai yaa	ຮ້ານຂາຍຢາ
phone	too'la'sap	ໂທລະສັບ
phone card	bat too'la'sap	ບັດໂທລະສັບ
phone number	(naam)ber too'la'sap	ນຳເບີໂທລະສັບ
photo	huup	ຮູບ
picture	huup paap	ຮູບພາບ
pick up a (person)	hap	ຮັບ
pillow	mawn	ໝອນ
pity	i'duu dton	ອິດູຕົນ
play (v)	lin	ຫຼິ້ນ
police	dtaam luat	ຕຳຫຼວດ
politics	gaan muhh'ang	ການເມືອງ
pool (swim)	sa'lawy naam	ສະລອຍນ້ຳ
poor	tuk (nyaak)	ທຸກ (ຍາກ)
popular	doong dang	ໂດ່ງດັ່ງ
pork	(siin) muu	(ຊີ້ນ) ໝູ
postcard	gak/phoot gaat	ກັກ/ໂພດກາດ
post office	paii'sa'nii	ໄປສະນີ
pray	paa wa naa	ພາວະນາ
prefer	mak laai gu'aa	ມັກຫຼາຍກວ່າ
president	pa taan pa'ayt	ປະທານປະເທດ
pretty	ngaam	ງາມ
private	su'an dtu'aa	ສ່ວນຕົນ
probably	baang tii	ບາງທີ
promise	san yaa	ສັນຍາ
public	saa tha' la'na son	ສາທາລະນະຊົນ
pull	duhng	ດຶງ
push	nyuu	ຍູ້
put	(ow) saii	(ເອົາ) ໃສ່

Q

quality	kun'na paai	ຄຸນນະພາຍ
quantity	pa li maan	ປະລິມານ
queen	laa si nii	ລະຊິນີ
quiet	(mit) ngiap/sa ngop	(ມິດ) ງຽບ/ສະງົບ
quit (job)	sao, la awwk	ເຊົ້າ/ລາອອກ

R

rabies	pen look waw	ເປັນໂລກວໍ້
racism	gaan lang giat phiu	ການລັງກຽດຜິວ
radio	wi ta nyu	ວິທະຍຸ
rash (n)	pen puhhn kan/hun han	ເປັນຜື່ນຄັນ/ຫຸມຫັນ
razor	miit thaae muat	ມິດແຖມວດ
read	aan	ອ່ານ
ready	pawm laae'o	ພ້ອມແຄ້ວ
real	taae jing	ແທ້ຈິງ
really?	maaen baww?	ແມ່ນບໍ?
receipt	bin	ບິນ
red	sii daaeng	ສີແດງ
relative (n)	nyaat dti pii nawng	ຍາດຕິພີ່ນ້ອງ
religion	saa sa'naa	ສາສະໜາ
remember	juhh (jam)	ຈື່ (ຈຳ)
rent	sow	ເຊົ້າ
reserve(v)	jawng waii/sa nguan waii	ຈອງໄວ້/ສະຫງວນໄວ້
respect	kow lop/nap thuhh	ເຄົາລົບ/ນັບຖື
retire	lii taai	ລີທາຍ
return	gap khuhhn	ກັບຄືນ
revolution	gaan pa dti wat	ການປະຕິວັດ
rich	hang/lu'ao	ຮັ່ງ/ລວຍ
ride	khii	ຂີ່
rightside	buhh'ang khuaa	ເບື້ອງຂວາ
right (correct)	thuhhk (dtawng)	ຖືກ (ຕ້ອງ)
river	maae naam	ແມ່ນ້ຳ
road	hon taang	ຫົນທາງ

room	hawng	ຫ້ອງ
run	laaen	ແລ່ນ
rush	(hiip) fhaao	(ຮີບ) ຟ້າວ

S

sad	sow	ເສົ້າ
safe (n)	pawt paii	ປອດໄພ
safe (adj)	waii jaii daii	ໄວ້ໃຈໄດ້
salary (monthly)	ng´n duhh'an	ເງິນເດືອນ
sale (v)	khaai	ຂາຍ
salt	guhh'a	ເກືອ
same	khuhh gaan/yaang di'ow gan	ຄືການ/ຍ່າງດຽວກັນ
save	hak saa	ຮັກສາ
say	wow	ເວົ້າ
scared	het haii dtok jaii/yaan	ເຮັດໃຫ້ຕົກໃຈ/ຢ້ານ
school	hoong hian	ໂຮງຮຽນ
science	wi ta nyaa saat	ວິທະຍາສາດ
scratch (v)	gao	ເກົາ
sea	ta'lay	ທະເລ
second	tii sawng	ທີສອງ
secret	ku'am lap	ຄວາມລັບ
see	hen	ເຫັນ
sell (v)	khaai	ຂາຍ
send	song (paii)	ສົ່ງ (ໄປ)
senseless	khaat sa dti/ngoo khow	ຂາດສະຕິ/ໂງ່ເຂົ້າ
serious	jing jang/sii liat	ຈິງຈັງ/ສີລຽດ
sew	nyip	ຫຍິບ
sex	payt/gaan	ເພດ/ການ
shampoo	saem puu	ແຊມພູ
share (v)	baaeng	ແບ່ງ
shave	thaae	ແຖ
shaving cream	foom thaae nu'at	ໂຟມແຖໜວດ
shoes	guhhp	ເກີບ
short (adj)	dtiaa/san	ເຕ້ຍ/ສັ້ນ

shower (n)	fak bu'aa	ฝักบัว
shy	(mii) aai	(มี) อาย
sick	khaii/baw sa'baai	ไข้/บໍ່ສະบาย
silk	maii	ไໝ
sing	hawng peng	ร้อງເพງ
sister	uhh'ai/nawg saao	ເอื้อย/บ้อງสาว
sit down	nang long	นั่งลໍງ
size	kha'naat	ຂະໜาด
slave	(khaa) taat	(ຂ้า) ทาด
sleep	nawn (lap)	นอน (ຫຼับ)
slow	saa	ຊ้า
small	nawy	น้อย
smart	goo/sa'laat	ໄກ้/ຊะຫຼาด
smell (v)	(daii) gin	(ได้) กิ่น
smells bad	men	ເໝັน
smells good	hawm	ຫอม
smoke (v)	suup	สูບ
smoke (n)	kuan	ຄວัน
snore	gon	ກ่น
snow	hi ma	ຫิมะ
soap	sa'buu	สะบู
soft	awwn (num)	อ่อน (ນ่ຸม)
soldier	ta haan	ทะຫาน
sometimes	baang way'laa	บาງເວลา
son	luuk saai	ลูกຊาย
sorry	siaa jaii/khaww toot	ເสยใจ/ຂໍໂทด
south	tit dtaii	ทิດໃต้
speak	wow	ເວ้า
spoon	buang	บ่อງ
sport	gi'laa	กิลา
stamp (n)	sa'dtaaem	สะແตມ
stand up	yuhhn khuhhn	ຢืนຂึ้น
stapler	ga'lap fherr	กะลับฟิ
start	luhhm dton	ເລີ່มຕ้น

stay	pak yuu	ພັກຢູ່
steal	(khii) lak	(ຂີ້)ລັກ
stingy	khii tii	ຂີ້ທີ
stop	yut/jawt	ຢຸດ/ຈອດ
store	gep waii/sa som	ເກັບໄວ້/ສະສົມ
strange	paaek (naa)	ແປກ(ໜ້າ)
street	tha'non	ຖະໜົນ
strong	khaaeng haaeng	ແຂງແຮງ
study	hian	ຮຽນ
sugar	naam dtaan	ນ້ຳຕານ
sun	dtaa wen	ຕາເວັນ
sure	naae nawn/man jaii	ແນ່ນອນ/ໝັ້ນໃຈ
surprised	het haii paaek jaii	ເຮັດໃຫ້ແປກໃຈ
swim	lawy naam	ລອຍນ້ຳ

T

table	dto	ໂຕະ
take	ow (paii)	ເອົາ(ໄປ)
talk	wow	ເວົ້າ
tall	suung	ສູງ
tape	sa gawt dtit	ສະກ໋ອດຕິດ
taste	sim (lot)	ຊິມ(ລົດ)
telecom center	suun too'la'sap	ສູນໂທລະສັບ
tell	bawk	ບອກ
temperature	un'na puum	ອຸນນະພູມ
temple	wat	ວັດ
that	nan/sing nan	ນັ້ນ/ສິ່ງນັ້ນ
there	yuu nan/tii nan	ຢູ່ນັ້ນ/ທີ່ນັ້ນ
they	pu'ak khow	ພວກເຂົາ
thing	sing khawng	ສິ່ງຂອງ
thirsty	hiu naam	ຫິວນ້ຳ
this	an'nii	ອັນນີ້
tissue	tiis'suu	ທິສຊູ
tie	mat	ມັດ

time	way'laa	ເວລາ
tire	yaang lot	ຢາງລົດ
tired	muhh'ai	ເມື່ອຍ
tofu	dtow huu	ເຕົ້າຮູ້
together	naam gan/huam gan	ນຳກັນ/ຮວມກັນ
toilet	hawng naam	ຫ້ອງນ້ຳ
tonight	muhh laaeng	ມື້ແລງ
too much	poot	ໂພດ
tourist	nak tawng ti'ow	ນັກທ່ອງທ່ຽວ
towel	phaa set dtoo	ຜ້າເຊັດໂຕ
traffic	fhaii daaeng	ໄຟແດງ
train	lot fhaii	ລົດໄຟ
translate	paae (kuaam)	ແປ (ຄວາມ)
travel	gaan derrn taang/	ການເດີນທາງ/
	tawng ti'ow	ທ່ອງທ່ຽວ
tree	dton maii	ຕົ້ນໄມ້
trust	waii jaii/suhh'a jaii	ໄວ້ໃຈ/ເຊື່ອໃຈ
try	pa nyaa nyaam	ພະຍາຍາມ
turn	liao	ລ້ຽວ

U		
ugly	khii laai	ຂີ້ລ້າຍ
umbrella	kan hom	ຄັນຮົ່ມ
U.N.	sa ha pa saa saat	ສະຫະປະຊາຊາດ
under	gawng/lum	ກ້ອງ/ລຸ່ມ
up	khuhhn paii/tuhng	ຂື້ນໄປ/ເທິງ
use (v)	saii	ໃຊ້

V		
vacant	waang	ວ່າງ
vague	kum kuhh'a/	ຄຸມເຄືອ/ບໍ່ແຈ້ງ
	bawjaaeng	
valuable	khawng mii kaa/pen	ຂອງມີຄ່າ/ເປັນລາຄາ
	laa'kaa	

vegetable (p. 53)	phak	ຜັກ
vegetarian	kon gin dtaae phak	ຄົນກິນແຕ່ຜັກ
very	laai (khuhhn)	ຫຼາຍ (ຂຶ້ນ)
video	wii'dii'oo	ວິດີໂອ
vinegar	naam som	ນ້ຳສົ້ມ
violent	hun haaeng/ hak hoom	ຮຸນແຮງ/ຫັກໂຫມ
visit	yiam yaam	ຢ້ຽມຢາມ
vocabulary	kaam sap	ຄຳສັບ
voice	siang	ສຽງ
volume	sa'bap	ສະບັບ
volunteer	aa saa sa'mak	ອາສາສະໝັກ
vote	awwk siang/long ka naaen	ອອກສຽງ/ລົງຄະແນນ

W

Wait	(laww) thaa	(ລໍ) ຖ້າ
wake up	dtuhhn khuhhn	ຕື່ນຂຶ້ນ
walk	nyaang	ຍ່າງ
wall	fhaa	ຝາ
want	yaak (daii)	ຢາກ (ໄດ້)
war	song kaam	ສົງຄາມ
wash	sak/ laang	ຊັກ/ລ້າງ
waste	sin puhh'ang	ຊິ້ນເປື້ອງ
watch (v)	buhng	ເບິ່ງ
watch (n)	moong	ໂມງ
water	naam duhhm	ນ້ຳດື່ມ
way	taang/wi thii taang	ທາງ/ວິທີທາງ
we	pu'ak how	ພວກເຮົ້າ
weak	awwn aae	ອ່ອນແອ
wealth	kuaam hang mii	ຄວາມຮັ່ງມີ
weapon	aa wut	ອາວຸດ
wear	nung/saii	ນຸ່ງ/ໃສ່
weather	aa'gaat	ອາກາດ
week	aa'tit	ອາທິດ

141

weekend	taai aa'tit	ທ້າຍອາທິດ
weird	pa laat/pen dtaa yaan	ປະຫຼາດ/ເປັນຕາຍ້ານ
west	tit dtaa wen dtok	ທິດຕາເວັນຕົກ
wet	biak	ປຽກ
what	maaen nyang	ແມ່ນຫຍັງ
whatever	maaen nyang gaww dtaam	ແມ່ນຫຍັງກໍຕາມ
when	muhh'a daii	ເມື່ອໃດ
where	yuu saii	ຢູ່ໃສ
whiskey	laao	ເຫຼົ້າ
whisper	suhm	ຊື່ມ
white	sii khow	ສີຂາວ
who	maaen phaii	ແມ່ນໃຜ
why	pen nyang	ເປັນຫຍັງ
wide	guaang	ກວ້າງ
wife	miaa	ເມຍ
wild	baa thuhh'an/	ບາເຖື່ອນ/
	hun haaeng	ຮຸນແຮງ
will	ja/si	ຈະ/ຊິ
win	sa'na	ຊະນະ
windy	lom haaeng	ລົມແຮງ
wine	laao waaeng	ເຫຼົ້າແວງ
wish	paat tha naa	ປາດຖະໜາ
with	gap	ກັບ
without	paat sa'jaak, baw saii	ປາດສະຈາກ/ບໍ່ໃສ່
woman	phuu nying	ຜູ້ຍິງ
wood	maii	ໄມ້
word	kaam wow	ຄຳເວົ້າ
work (v)	het wiak	ເຮັດວຽກ
world	look	ໂລກ
worry	pen hu'ang/gang won	ເປັນຫ່ວງ/ກັງວົນ
worse	su'aa gu'aa	ຊົ່ວກວ່າ
worst	su'aa tii sut/	ຊົ່ວທີ່ສຸດ/
	baww dii tii sut	ບໍ່ດີທີ່ສຸດ
write	khian	ຂຽນ

writer	phuu khian/	ຜູ້ຂຽນ/
	nak khian	ນັກຂຽນ
wrong	phit	ຜິດ

X

xenophobia	kon tii sang dtaang pa'tayt	ຄົນທີ່ຊັງຕ່າງປະເທດ
x-ray	gaan saai saaeng	ການສາຍແສງ

Y

yard	derrn baan	ເດີນບ້ານ
yawn	how nawn	ຫາວນອນ
year	pii	ປີ
yell	hawng dang dang, hawng saii	ຮ້ອງດັງໆ, ຮ້ອງໃສ່
yellow	sii luhh'ang	ສີເຫລືອງ
yes	jow. err. doy. dooy kha nawy	ເຈົ້າ. ເອີ. ໂດຍ. ໂດຍອະນ້ອຍ
yesterday	muhh waan'nii	ມື້ວານນີ້
you	jow/pu'ak jow	ເຈົ້າ/ພວກເຈົ້າ

Z

zipper	sip	ຊິບ
zoo	su'an sat	ສວນສັດ

Cultural Differences?

1. Smiling goes a long way.
2. Confrontation does not.
3. Ask before taking photos of people.
4. Take your shoes off when necessary.
5. Hand over things instead of throwing them.
6. Keep the noise down.
7. Do not sit on desks.
8. Do not point at people.
9. Do not touch things, animals or people with your feet.
10. Do not direct the bottom of your feet at people.
11. Duck your head a bit when passing or walking between people.
12. Do not sit higher than old people unless invited to. If they are on the floor, sit on the floor too, not on a chair.
13. Do not step over people when they are lying or sitting on the floor.
14. Do not blow your nose in public.
15. Do not spit.
16. Appear clean and dress modestly.

Thank you very much
ຂອບໃຈຫລາຍໆ

Thank you Souphing for agreeing to work with me on this mon-
strosity. Without you I would have never been able to start
this project. Without your difficult handwriting to deci-
pher, I would have never learned to read hand-written Lao;
without your translations I'd still be fumbling through a
dictionary; and without your typing skills I would still be
typing.

Thank you Tee. If it weren't for you I would never have
finished this book. You made me work when I was tired of looking at the screen, and you deserve a medal for all that you added
in its final stages.

Thanks to my mate Simon for always ragging on me for my
style, arguing with me about nothing and always answering my
question, "What was I talking about?" with "I don't know."

Thanks Liam for letting me interrupt you during your horror
movies with stupid questions like "Which is friend and which is
pig again?"

Thank you Suzie for giving this book its first harsh edit and
being home in my time of need.

Thanks Mike for making it to Laos, for putting some good
ideas into this book, and for your constant supply of good BS.
And to think you once said I never did anything for you! You
made the credits my boy.

Thank you Lang for introducing me to the massage palace and being such a close friend all these years. Your humor and generosity never failed me.

Thank you Shelby for your wild side and superb parties.

Thanks Carrie for your ceaseless spirit and your faith in my driving skills.

Thanks Wendy for sticking my fist in your mouth and showing me the alien trick.

Thanks Leisa for always being up to a full-on discussion about something. In Tyler I trust.

Thanks Cliff for your never-ending supply of energy and eagerness to do just about anything.

Thanks Paul for discussing GM foods and Burma in Nong Khai that night. I'm sure those talks played a role in this book somehow.

Thanks Carolyn and Adrianne for the Vynysty Party. I still can't get the oil out of my chest hair.

Thanks Nick, Rome, Aling, PJ and everyone at the Image Bar for all the long nights and fine tunes.

Thanks Air Noy for your language tutorials in real Lao.

Thank you Pic and Bawk for your Lao lessons, always being together, and climbing the tree in my front yard to get fruit.

Thanks Somsonouk for letting me crash at your place when I first arrived in Lao.

Thanks Dic and Nui, wherever you are, for just being Dic and Nui.

Thanks Diana and Owen for taking a copy of this book to edit and never doing anything with it.

Thanks Angela for telling me to make sure tofu made the dictionary.

Thanks Ely for putting up with my mess all over your desk all the time. Come to think of it, thanks for putting up with me all of the time. You were a great flat-mate, and you fed me well.

Thanks Lot for your suggestions. To think that there is a little bit of Belgium in this Lao book is kind of weird, but without you there would be no pink.

Thanks to all my students and bosses at VIS, the U.S. embassy, and the Mekong Fisheries for being such fun, so interesting, and most of all for teaching me so much about Laos.

Thanks to all my friends who made it over to visit me in Laos. Even if you had nothing to do with this book, it was a joy showing you what a superb country this is.

Thanks to my parents for over thirty years of encouragement and inspiration. And thank you for visiting me all over the world. If it weren't for you two, I wouldn't be here at all. And neither would this book.